SYBEX

OFFICIAL
strategies & secrets™

S0-ABA-582

ZOO TYCOON 2®

Michael Rymaszewski

SYBEX®

SAN FRANCISCO • LONDON

PUBLISHER: DAN BRODNITZ

PRINT PRODUCTION MANAGER: RACHEL BOYCE

ACQUISITIONS AND
DEVELOPMENTAL EDITOR: WILLEM KNIBBE

PRODUCTION EDITOR: PATRICK CUNNINGHAM

EDITOR: CANDACE ENGLISH

BOOK PRODUCTION: SUSAN HONEYWELL

COVER DESIGN: VICTOR ARRE, RGRAPHICS

POSTER DESIGN: KEVIN BROWN

CHAPTER OPENER DESIGN: LOU A. CATANZARO

DIRECTOR OF CONTRACTS
AND LICENSING: MONICA BAUM

Library of Congress Control Number: 2003102932

ISBN: 0-7821-4357-1

Manufactured in the United States of America

10 9 8 7 6 5 4 3 2 1

Acknowledgments

This book became a book thanks to many different people. As usual, I owe a debt of gratitude to the Sybex team: Willem Knibbe, whose deft handling of this project ensured its successful conclusion; Candace English, whose eagle-eyed editing made this book more readable; and Patrick Cunningham, who patiently made sure everything fit together the way it should.

This guide became a good guide thanks to the help of many people at Microsoft Game Studios and Blue Fang Games. At Microsoft, Kiki McMillan made sure we got what we needed and, together with Val Miller, provided excellent feedback on all the chapters; Kevin Brown designed the handsome poster that came with this book and supplied the art decorating its pages. At Blue Fang Games, Senior Designers Bart Simon and Linda Currie reviewed chapters and set me straight on many issues; extra thanks go to Bart for finding the time to explain the arcane inner workings of the game. A separate thanks goes to Lou Catanzaro at Blue Fang for designing the chapter-opener images. Thank you all, folks! It's been a great ride.

Contents

CHAPTER 3

MAKING PEOPLE HAPPY 42

CHAPTER 4

CARING FOR ANIMALS 56

CHAPTER 5

THE ANIMALS WITHIN 74

CHAPTER 6

FREEFORM AND CHALLENGE GAMES . . 108

CHAPTER 7

CAMPAIGN GAMES 130

APPENDIX A

ANIMAL, BIOME OBJECT, AND BIOME COMPATIBILITY DATA 184

APPENDIX **B**

BUILDINGS, STRUCTURES, AND OBJECTS BY FAME. 192

APPENDIX **C**

CHALLENGES. 198

INTRODUCTION

This strategy guide sheds light on many of *Zoo Tycoon 2*'s hidden aspects, investigates the mysterious workings of zoo guests and animals, and offers a lot of practical advice on playing a winning game. You should find it helpful regardless of what you choose to play—a Campaign scenario, a Freeform game, or a Challenge game.

The guide begins with a general game overview in **Chapter 1**, which also contains advice on getting started on the right foot. **Chapter 2** reviews the basic tycoon skills: it discusses planning, building, and running your zoo, along with zoo finances. It also contains practical tips for using the game's powerful terrain-modifying tools.

Chapter 3 turns the spotlight on the people who give you money: zoo guests. It discusses who they are and what makes them happy, and gives plenty of practical advice on putting them into a blissful state. **Chapter 4** focuses on animal care, reviewing animal needs and advising you on ways to make your zoo animals happier. You'll find even more tips on animal happiness in **Chapter 5**, which discusses every single animal in the game, with the exception of the squirrels that inhabit many zoos (they make you no money, after all). The animal portraits in Chapter 5 are arranged by fame level, beginning with the species that are available at half-star fame.

Chapters 6 and 7 focus on gameplay. Chapter 6 examines the differences between Freeform and Challenge games and offers suggestions on making game choices fit your game goals. It concludes with a walkthrough for a winning opening when playing an extra-tough Challenge game, and advice on winning photo-safari and game challenges. Chapter 7 deals exclusively with the Campaign game. You'll find detailed walkthroughs for each *ZT2* scenario; many of these contain advice that is also helpful in Freeform and Challenge games.

At the very end of the guide, you'll find a set of four **appendices**. These contain important game data and a list of challenges, as well as tips from game insiders at Blue Fang and Microsoft Game Studios.

Don't forget to check the Sybex website, www.sybex.com, for more *Zoo Tycoon 2* information! We plan to post late-breaking game info, more game stats, and a review of patches (if there are any).

We hope you'll find this guide both enjoyable and useful. If you have any comments, please feel free to share them with us at www.sybex.com.

GETTING TO KNOW THE NEW TYCOON

THIS CHAPTER OFFERS A BROAD OVERVIEW OF WHAT *ZOO TYCOON 2* IS ABOUT. IT COMPLEMENTS AND EXPANDS ON THE INFORMATION IN THE GAME MANUAL. FOR NEWCOMERS TO *ZOO TYCOON*, WE'VE EXPLAINED HOW THE GAME WORKS, AND WHAT KIND OF MOVES WILL WORK FOR YOU. THE DIFFERENCES BETWEEN THE ORIGINAL AND THE SEQUEL ARE HIGHLIGHTED HERE FOR *ZOO TYCOON* VETERANS. THE CHAPTER CONCLUDES WITH COMMENTS ON THE GAME TUTORIALS AND ADVICE FOR MAKING THE GAME RUN BETTER.

ZOO TYCOON 2 SHARES THE SAME GAME PREMISE AS THE ORIGINAL: CREATE A SUCCESSFUL ZOO. BUT IN MANY DRAMATIC RESPECTS, ZT2 IS A NEW GAME. THE FIRST-PERSON VIEW LETS YOU WALK AROUND YOUR ZOO AND PERFORM THE FUNCTIONS OF A ZOOKEEPER, MAINTENANCE WORKER, OR ZOO PHOTOGRAPHER—ABILITIES THAT ARE FUN, BUT ALSO CARRY STRATEGIC IMPLICATIONS. ALTHOUGH THE ORIGINAL AND THE SEQUEL HAVE SIMILAR GAME GOALS, *ZOO TYCOON 2* INTRODUCES THE CONCEPT OF ZOO FAME: THE YARDSTICK USED TO MEASURE YOUR SUCCESS. EVEN THE INTERFACE IS RADICALLY DIFFERENT— A STRONG HINT FOR *ZOO TYCOON* VETERANS THAT SOME CHANGES IN THINKING WILL BE NEEDED TO SUCCEED IN ZT2. ARE YOU READY FOR CHANGE?

LET'S BEGIN WITH WHAT WE ALL LIKE A LOT: FAME.

BECOMING A BIG NAME

In *Zoo Tycoon 2*, fame is big. It's not only a measure of your zoo's success—it actually *defines* your zoo's success. After all, zoo fame is what lets you adopt increasingly exotic animals, the very animals you need to achieve even bigger fame for your zoo. It goes like this: you focus on making your first animals as happy as possible. Then you focus on making your first zoo guests as happy as possible. This will bring an increase in fame, resulting in new animals for adoption. You adopt these, and focus on making them as happy as possible.

A zoo's increase in fame brings other benefits, ranging from practical (you can charge guests more if you feel so inclined) to aesthetic (the entrance to your zoo gets a makeover—see Figure 1.1).

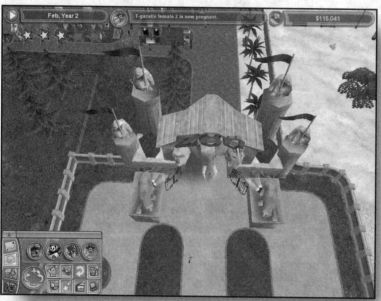

FIGURE 1.1:

A three-star makeover for your zoo entrance.

Acquiring adoption rights to new animal species is a big part of the game. Therefore, note that you can gain access to a new species by turning down one of the species currently on offer. To turn down a species, select it and click the button directly under the animal sex buttons on the animal-adoption panel. The rejected species disappears from the panel, and is replaced by a ghost image of the species that will be offered in its place once the progress bar below the ghost image is full. After you've succeeded in making an animal species breed in your zoo, make sure you switch that animal for a new species on the animal-adoption panel! See Chapter 5 for more details on obtaining adoption rights to new species.

Becoming really famous isn't simple—it requires you to excel in many different areas all at once. You'll have to pretty much equal the immortal Elvis to gain five-star fame. Here are the components of fame as listed in the game manual, and descriptions of what they mean in gameplay terms:

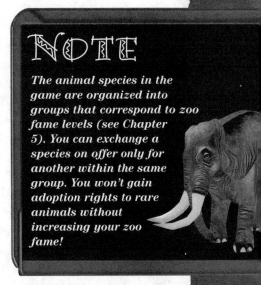

NOTE

The animal species in the game are organized into groups that correspond to zoo fame levels (see Chapter 5). You can exchange a species on offer only for another within the same group. You won't gain adoption rights to rare animals without increasing your zoo fame!

- 🐾 **Diversity of species**. To reach maximum fame, your zoo must contain at least 25 of the 30 animal species in the game, and all these animals have to be deliriously happy. It's easier to hit maximum fame if you have more than 25 animal species represented in your zoo; having all 30 species is best. They don't have to be delirious with happiness then—very, very happy is good enough.

- 🐾 **Releasing animals into the wild.** You must breed animals in your zoo before you can release them into the wild in numbers significant enough to max out this contribution to zoo fame. To make animals breed, you have to make them happy. Yes, happiness strikes again.

- 🐾 **Completing scenario goals and challenges.** Animal happiness often plays an important role in completing scenario goals and challenges. How are you going to take that photo of an animal baby with its mother? Only if the animals in your zoo are comfortable enough to multiply. This category is inactive when playing a game in Freeform mode.

- 🐾 **Awards.** If the animals in your zoo aren't happy, the only award you can count on is the 100th Guest Attendance ribbon—provided you set zoo admission to Free. This category is inactive when playing a Campaign scenario.

- 🐾 **Guest happiness.** Your guests won't be happy if the animals aren't happy. In order to reach maximum guest happiness, you must also strive to meet your guests' personal needs—including catering to individual food and animal-viewing preferences if possible.

As you can see, there is only one road that leads to success in *Zoo Tycoon 2*: the joyful road of happiness for everyone. Chapters 3 and 4 contain plenty of info on how to make zoo guests and animals happy (you'll also find some extra happiness tips in Chapters 2 and 5).

Why Happiness Means Money

The insidious effect of happiness in *Zoo Tycoon 2* extends even to the unemotional realm of finance. That's right; in *ZT2*, happiness makes you money, just like that. Guest donations constitute the vast majority of your zoo's income, and guests donate money when the animals they are viewing are happy. When the guests are very happy themselves, they donate even more money—many guests will run to the nearest ATM to get some if they feel the money they have isn't enough.

Chapter 3 explains in detail what makes people happy, but the following is a brief summary of what puts the smileys over the guests' heads, and money in your donation boxes:

- **Happy animals.** If you watch the zoo guests, you'll see a sea of smileys followed by small stampedes toward the donations boxes when your animals demonstrate playful, happy behavior in exhibits that re-create their native habitats faithfully.

- **Need satisfaction.** Your guests have needs—boy, do they have needs. Let it be said that one of the most important zoo buildings is the luxury lavatory, or family restroom. The zoo concessions—big moneymakers in the original game—serve mainly to keep guests happy. Profits from concessions, although not insignificant, will never amount to more than a small fraction of your zoo's income. *Zoo Tycoon* veterans should also note that in *ZT2*, guest amusement is a distinct need.

- **New knowledge.** The zoo guests in *Zoo Tycoon 2* are a knowledge-hungry lot. The importance of this noble guest need is underscored by the special smiley that appears whenever a zoo guest feels educated. Zoo guests gain new knowledge not in your zoo's restaurants and hamburger joints, but exclusively through watching zoo animals perform certain actions and by listening to educators. Watch the donation boxes get busy following certain behaviors!

- **Zoo beauty.** We all love beauty, and dislike ugliness. Zoo guests are much happier in a beautiful zoo (good exhibit design is particularly important!). *ZT2* offers you the option of walking down the paths of your own zoo and seeing first-hand what things look like. Certain Campaign scenarios and $5,000 Challenge games will force you to roll up your sleeves and deal with beauty's number-one enemy: trash. Zoo guests are deeply distressed by trash, and the smart tycoon will vigilantly monitor trash can and recycling bin capacity, hiring enough maintenance workers to keep the zoo spotless.

The single-minded focus on happiness in *ZT2* doesn't mean it's an easy game. This is because any search for happiness is complex by nature, and happiness in-game is subject to many different influences. Your role in the game is to identify those influences and modify them for the better. Examples: Your lion's habitat may need an extra swipe with the grass-and-dirt Savannah biome brush. An extra couple of benches may need to be placed just so. You may need to step into first-person view to help out your zookeepers—even the greatest tycoon will occasionally have to stoop to clean animal poop and pick up trash. This first-person-view, hands-on activity is a necessity in all Challenge games with $5,000 starting money. As they say, it builds character (see Figure 1.2).

> ### NOTE
>
> *The big secret of making money in ZT2 is to ignore making money, and spend all you've got on making everyone happy—starting with the animals. You'll quickly find the green stuff coming in faster than you can spend it. Chapter 2 has specific advice and tips to get you going down the road of the benevolent tycoon.*

Press space bar to clean up the Ungulate Poop

FIGURE 1.2:

Many green tycoons will see this message in their dreams.

The road to happiness in *ZT2* starts with careful planning. If you don't design your zoo well, you might run into all sorts of trouble that can render efforts to increase guest happiness null and void. A simple mistake such as placing a restroom in a spot where its entrance makes people line up in other people's way can result in the most horrific traffic jams. The game manual has two pages full of excellent tips on zoo design (if you still haven't read the manual, go do it now). The section below adds some extra pointers, and you'll also find design info in Chapter 2 (zoo layout, building/exhibit placement), Chapter 3 (guest amenity placement), and Chapter 4 (exhibit design).

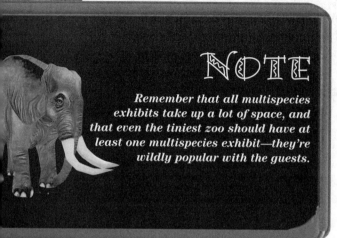

NOTE

Remember that all multispecies exhibits take up a lot of space, and that even the tiniest zoo should have at least one multispecies exhibit—they're wildly popular with the guests.

BUILDING AND RUNNING YOUR ZOO

The building you'll do depends on the kind of game you play. Campaign-scenario games have their own special requirements (Chapter 7 has the details), but there is always one primary consideration when planning your zoo: the size of the map.

You won't have much of a choice when playing a small map; small maps more or less dictate the zoo layout once you've estimated how many exhibits you're going to fit in. However, the plot thickens with medium and large maps, and *ZT2* rewards unorthodox solutions in zoo design. Modifying the terrain (creating mountains, valleys, etc.) is absolutely free of charge. This makes inventive solutions to zoo and exhibit design very feasible. You can make your zoo much more attractive to guests *plus* save some serious cash on fencing by building sunken exhibits, or enclosing exhibits with moats and cliffs. The new interface makes terrain modifications extra-easy, although the tools might take some getting used to; it's best to practice with the game paused or in the Freeform mode, where money and mistakes don't matter.

Zoo Tycoon veterans should note that *ZT2* offers new, greater flexibility in terms of effective zoo layout. Chapter 2 offers layout suggestions depending on map size (small, medium, large). New players should pay attention to the manual's zoo-design tips! The grid pattern described there is the safest bet for inexperienced players, and works well on small maps.

PLACING BUILDINGS AND CREATING EXHIBITS

As in the original *Zoo Tycoon*, not all buildings and animal exhibits are equal; some have considerably more pull with the public than the others. An exhibit featuring a biome with many species, or a truly rare animal, will always fascinate many guests. The attractiveness of each of the game's animals is discussed in Chapter 5. For now, keep in mind that exhibits with strong pull act as zoo-traffic regulators. Placing a highly attractive exhibit at the end of a zoo path ensures good traffic flow along that path. The same rule applies to guest amenities and amusement structures: some are more attractive than others. You'll find more information on strategic exhibit and zoo-structure placement in Chapters 2 and 3.

> **TIP**
>
> *Check out the Biome Squares map (available both under Challenge and Freeform games). It's a great example of the inventive zoo-design solutions made possible by the new, free-of-charge terrain-modification options.*

> **TIP**
>
> *Remember that all animals have privacy needs, and that not all species can use a shelter! This can be particularly troublesome with sunken exhibits, which are viewed by guests standing on a higher elevation. You may have to employ natural barriers to the guests' line of sight, such as hills or rows of trees, and/or use solid fencing such as brick walls to give your animals the privacy they need.*

The ability to create great exhibits is the mark of a successful tycoon. It isn't such an easy ability to acquire, because you must show plenty of foresight. Your ultimate goal will always be to create a multispecies or at least multianimal exhibit (a pair of adult animals with baby animals). If you cannot afford to build a suitably large exhibit right away, you must allow for its future painless expansion. Guests get big kicks out of seeing flawlessly re-created biomes that display a variety of terrain, rocks, and plant life in addition to animal life.

Pay special attention when building your first few exhibits and using the biome brush to create a suitable habitat for your chosen animal(s). Selecting any biome opens a set of terrain choices, ranging from wooded areas to water (see Figure 1.3). "Painting" the habitat with the default biome brush costs no money; however, if you select one of the options that features plants, rocks, and trees, you will be charged for any such objects placed by the biome brush. It's simplest to paint the entire habitat with the no-cost biome brushes of your choice (dirt, sand, forest floor, etc.) before you switch to a brush that places objects. You'll find detailed advice on exhibit design in Chapters 4 and 5.

FIGURE 1.3:
You can always apply the default biome brush free of charge. Treat it as primer, and apply it over the entire exhibit area.

RUNNING (AROUND) YOUR ZOO

Zoo Tycoon 2 lets you monitor your zoo on several levels. As shown in the manual, you'll access various important screens through buttons on the main game screen.

The View Quick Stats button is the one you'll use most to monitor your zoo. The tabs on the Quick Stats screen let you switch between lists of zoo animals, guests, and employees at a single click; bad news is highlighted in red. Clicking on an animal, guest, or employee icon locks the overhead camera view onto your selection.

The View Finances button is likely to get a workout in the opening stages of a game. As time goes on and money comes gushing in an ever-increasing

stream, you'll be less concerned about money and more concerned about what to spend it on. You'll be checking the Zoo Fame and Scenario Goals/Challenges screens regularly throughout the game, but the experienced tycoon will eventually be able to foretell a fame increase simply by monitoring the Quick Stats screen and ongoing zoo action in the overhead view. Note that you always get a message when your zoo's fame increases, but you *don't* get a message when it decreases.

NOTE

If you're new to the Zoo Tycoon series, remember that you can also view zoo finances by clicking on the zoo gate.

Chapter 2 details all the organizational challenges you'll face in your rise to glory. But in addition to being well-organized, the smart tycoon is always in the right place at the right time. He moves around the map efficiently, and manipulates zoom levels and views to best effect. Scrolling in the overhead view can be a slow process, so use the Overview Map to quickly jump between hotspots.

The first-person view is used for both work and pleasure. It allows you to stroll around the zoo as a carefree guest, and lets you perform the duties of a zookeeper and maintenance worker. At certain points in a game, performing these duties may be a necessity. A $5,000 Challenge game will make you count pennies and save on staff salaries for the first couple of months; a tight Campaign scenario may force you to move faster than any of your employees; a very big zoo can often have more emergencies than zoo staff can handle at a given time. To perform the duties of a zoo employee efficiently, don't switch to first-person view until you've located the problem. A big multispecies biome can have you running yourself ragged in search of the elusive poop. It's much more effective to scan the exhibit by staying in the overhead view and zooming in fairly close, then scrolling around. This lets you parachute into first-person view in exactly in the right spot, too.

NOTE

Use the filters for guests, foliage, buildings, and fences to hide these features, making it easier to spot the animals or animal poop you're looking for.

You'll find more in-depth advice on playing as the zookeeper and maintenance worker in Chapter 2. Now let's take a look at one of the most charming features of the game: the camera view.

THE PHOTO SAFARI, OR CAMERA VIEW IN CLOSE-UP

Like the first-person view, the camera view in the game is meant to be used for both pleasure and purpose. You may collect a photo album full of funny shots—or you can take on the game's photo challenges. You'll encounter photo challenges when playing in the Challenge mode or in some of the game's Campaign scenarios.

Challenges, ways of completing them swiftly, and the resulting rewards are discussed in Chapter 6 and Appendix C. Here, let's look at some mechanics of taking pictures.

The camera view does not let you pass through gates (front zoo gates included) or open exhibit gates. Moving around your zoo in camera view is a lot of fun; but, as in real life, you won't find a lot of good pictures to take that way. When you're hunting for a specific photograph—be it part of a challenge or for fun—it's best to move around in the overhead view with a medium-close zoom. This view lets you quickly identify fleeting opportunities (for example, "Aha! That zebra looks like it's going to, er, use an enrichment object.") Once you notice an opportunity to take a fun or challenge-scoring photograph, quickly zoom in on the spot where you intend to stand, switch to camera view, and hit the space bar to take the picture (see Figure 1.4).

FIGURE 1.4:

Capturing certain images means being quick on the trigger.

Remember to empty your camera (it's best to have at least five out of the 10 available shots left at all times) and reorganize your photo album periodically—its contents carry over from game to game, and may cause confusion if you're switching between saved games.

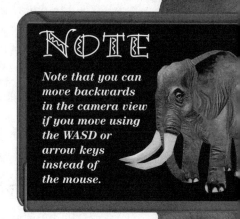

Sharing Your Pictures

Zoo Tycoon 2 lets you export the pictures you've taken into HTML format and share them with other *ZT2* players over the Internet. Here's what to do:

1. Open the photo album while in the game.

2. Click the Export Photo Album to HTML button.

3. Name your album file and save it to your hard drive—you might want to create a special folder.

4. Send the folder with the album to your friends. (Compress it first with WinZip or another utility for safer and quicker transfer.)

If you're clever and know HTML well, you can also post the photo album as a Web page. Of course, being clever and knowing HTML well means you don't need any advice.

Getting Ready to Play

The first step to enjoying *Zoo Tycoon 2* is making sure it runs well on your system. Although you can certainly play *ZT2* on a minimum-specs system, you should know that it is a demanding game: It's best if you treat the system *recommended* in the game specs as the *minimum* system for playing *ZT2*. This is for two reasons. The first is that although *ZT2* can be played at a resolution as low as 800 × 600, it is truly beautiful at the higher resolutions (available through the Game Options panel). The higher the resolution, the more beauty you'll see; treat 1024 × 768 with medium detail as the minimum for getting a respectable amount of eye candy. If you find performance suffering, select the Low Video Details setting on the Game Options menu and lower the resolution.

The second reason for the demanding system requirements is that you, of course, want to build the best zoo in the world. And the best zoo in the world is going to be a very big zoo, with over 100 animals and 120 guests (up to a dozen or so more when zoo attendance is boosted by winning a special challenge—see Appendix C). This is a heavy load to handle for any system, and you might be forced to pause the game during such precision operations as creating a new exhibit or laying down a new path network.

Of course, it goes without saying that your computer is regularly serviced, the hard drive is defragmented, your sound and video card drivers are up-to-date, and you aren't running other applications in the background while playing *ZT2*. If your computer hasn't seen any servicing since day one, it's high time you opened Windows Help and read the entry about the Maintenance Wizard.

Once you and your machine are ready for action, the first thing you should do is play the tutorials.

TUTORIAL NOTES

The tutorials are what tutorials should be—completely self-explanatory. However, being the most alert tycoon candidate to ever walk this earth, you should take special note of a few things:

- In the second tutorial, note the size of the elephant shelter. If you needed extra proof that *ZT2* is about building *big* exhibits, this is it.

- In the third tutorial, make a point of navigating around the zoo using the map view, the overhead view, the guest (first-person) view, and the Photo Safari (camera) view. Don't forget to shoot a roll of film while you're at it!

- The third tutorial teaches you how to build food and drink stands. You don't get to build a restroom, but remember this for all future games: you should always build a restroom before any other guest amenity (guest service building).

- After playing the tutorial, you may want to play a few Freeform games. This will let you get used to the interface and discover the full wealth of options available in *Zoo Tycoon 2*. You'll find more info on Freeform (and Challenge) games in Chapter 6.

The next chapter discusses your role in the game, and explains what you have to do to become a successful tycoon.

HOW TO BECOME RICH AND FAMOUS

Every true tycoon is rich and famous. This chapter should help you reach this happy status by unveiling some of the secrets of success in *Zoo Tycoon 2*. Not all the secrets; guests and animals are exposed for who they are in the next three chapters, and you'll find plenty of advice in other chapters, too. This chapter focuses on basic tycoon skills. It discusses how to plan and lay out a zoo, manage zoo finances and staff, and even handle poop and trash in a graceful and efficient manner. The all-important skill of caring for animals is discussed on its own in Chapter 4.

Please note that much of the advice in this chapter is of little use in Freeform games, in which unlimited cash lets you ignore game finances completely. Freeform games also let you hire an army of zookeepers and maintenance workers and build anything you want right away. Fame becomes incidental, since all animals can be adopted at half-star fame. However, this chapter will give you a deeper understanding of what goes on in your Freeform game, and you should find its advice pretty useful when playing Challenge games and Campaign scenarios.

THE TYCOON AS ZOO PLANNER AND BUILDER

While playing the game, you'll be spending plenty of time building exhibits and pathways, and placing guest amenities, zoo decor, and other zoo objects. All this building activity can be truly successful only if it's preceded by appropriate planning. However, it's a fact that many tycoons become impulsive when in possession of big amounts of cash. If this happens to you, and you find yourself on the verge of a building spree, ask yourself these three questions:

- Why do I want to build this? A lot of the time, the true answer is "Because I can." That's perfectly all right, but it doesn't do much for a tycoon's professional image. What's more, if you ask yourself this question every time you want to build something, you'll sometimes discover that your original choice doesn't make sense, but something else does. It's funny how often you might set out to place a hot-looking new food stand, and end up placing a much-needed family restroom instead.

- Where do I want to build this? You should ask yourself this question even if you've already picked the right spot (see Figure 2.1). A lot of the time, you'll find there's a slightly better spot after all. Every time you ask yourself this question, your zoo-layout skill will undergo a tiny improvement.

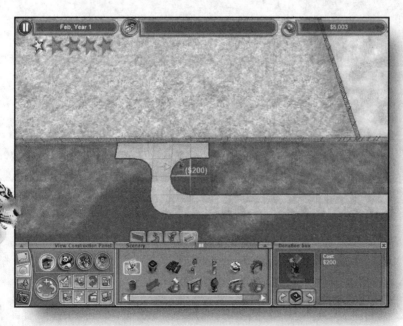

FIGURE 2.1:

Here or there? Placing a donation box in just the right spot is one of the most important tycoon skills.

How do I want to build this? This applies to exhibits and pathways—zoo structures and objects aren't built; they're placed ready-made on the map. Building good exhibits and efficient path networks is very important in the game. Note that this chapter deals solely with building exhibits; creating habitats in the exhibits is discussed in Chapters 4 and 5.

To enjoy the most success as a builder, you must precede any construction with proper planning. The section below on planning your zoo complements the game-manual info, referring to it when necessary.

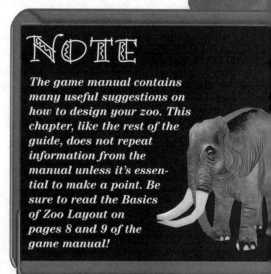

NOTE

The game manual contains many useful suggestions on how to design your zoo. This chapter, like the rest of the guide, does not repeat information from the manual unless it's essential to make a point. Be sure to read the Basics of Zoo Layout on pages 8 and 9 of the game manual!

Zoo-Layout Principles

Good zoo-layout solutions vary according to map size. A layout that works great on a small map won't work on a medium or large map. However, no matter what the size of the map, a few general zoo-layout principles apply every time you build a new zoo. The manual lists a few of them. Perhaps the most important is that top zoo attractions should be placed in the back of your zoo. When building a new zoo in *ZT2*, it's very helpful to think about it in terms of the front half and the back or rear half. The front half of your zoo is where much of the early zoo development will take place. But ultimately, the late-game exhibits that you build in the rear half will decide if your zoo is a five-star success. Always keep this in mind.

In general, treat the game manual's Top Ten Zoo Layout Tips and other zoo-design info as your 10 zoo-design commandments, with the following exceptions and considerations:

The fork layout, in which the central pathway running the length of the zoo consists of two separate lanes, needs more space between the lanes than suggested in the manual. The two-to-five-tiles divider width worked well in the original *Zoo Tycoon*, but you need at least half a dozen tiles, and preferably around 10, in *Zoo Tycoon 2*. You need the space for guest seating (picnic and umbrella tables). This makes the fork useful only on larger maps. Consider widening the divider to 12 or 14 tiles, and putting small single-specimen exhibits there wherever guest service buildings aren't needed. Use high, solid fencing to ensure the animals inside get enough privacy in spite of the heavy traffic.

The pathways in *ZT2* needn't be as wide as suggested in the manual. A path two tiles wide can handle the heaviest zoo traffic possible, as long as you don't place any objects on it (such as benches or trash cans). Less-frequented paths can be only one tile wide as long as there are no obstructions. Remember that you should always place guest service buildings off to the side of the pathway. Otherwise, a guest lineup may block traffic no matter how wide you make the path.

Another important principle is that guests like a mix of service buildings in the same area. Building your initial hot dog stand and soda stand far apart doesn't make sense, and they should have both trash cans and guest seating (picnic and/or umbrella tables) nearby. Locating the nearest restroom far away from the food and the drink doesn't make sense either, unless you're cruel by nature and want to sacrifice guest happiness in order to satisfy your sadistic urges. You should strive to create guest service areas in which a mix of guest amenities keeps visitors happy. The guest service buildings and structures that are exempt from this rule are listed on the next page.

> # TIP
>
> *Use the "second tile" rule whenever placing a guest service building alongside a zoo path. Always build on the second tile away from the path (or farther). A tile of space between the building and the path will allow a few guests to line up without disrupting the traffic.*

FIGURE 2.2:

Plenty of stuffed animals and silly hats for everyone!

- The restroom. This means both restroom types; small restrooms continue to be good at servicing awkward areas of your zoo even after the family model makes an appearance. Their size lets you fit them in easily almost anywhere.

- The gift cart. Put one in front of every exhibit (see Figure 2.2). For rarer animals, place a gift shop nearby that sells items that show off that particular animal.

- Benches. A bench near every animal-viewing area will make sure your guests will tirelessly continue touring your zoo. You can even place benches right up against the exhibit fence so that guests can watch animals and rest at the same time.

- Snack and dessert carts. These can and should be moved around, especially after you build your first restaurant, which also sells desserts.

- Bouncy rides. Bouncy rides are small enough to fit anywhere, and work very nicely when spread around the zoo. Putting a bouncy ride near a popular exhibit is a good move.

- Zoo decor. Beauty is beautiful anywhere, but you should make a point of beautifying high- and medium-traffic areas. These invariably include all crossroads and all restrooms.

TIP

When the number of guests in your zoo exceeds 60, start placing extra donation boxes in busy spots.

SELECTING ZOO LAYOUT TYPE

This is where map size comes in as the primary consideration. The smaller the map, the fewer choices you have. A zoo built on a small map has to squeeze maximum use out of every single tile of space if it's to reach five-star fame. Your best bet is a tight grid layout, as described in the manual, with guest service buildings spread out over the zoo. Alternatively, reserve an exhibit-sized area right in the center of the zoo for a consolidated guest service area. Place an extra restroom in each corner of your small zoo, plus a gift cart in front of each exhibit, but pack almost all remaining guest amenities into the central location. The shorter distances guests have to walk in a small zoo make this layout a good solution, but it won't work on larger maps!

Medium maps allow you a lot of leeway when selecting a zoo layout type. The grid will work here, but so will other concepts. The High Street is an approach that works well on medium maps: the majority of guest amenities are lined up along a wide central path that stretches from the entrance right to the back of the zoo. You can also build two dedicated guest service areas in the front and rear halves of your zoo, stretching them sideways as you add new guest service structures. Alternatively, a triangle-shaped pattern works. Your initial guest service area is placed in the center and close to the zoo entrance. Two smaller guest areas are added later, one near each far corner of the zoo.

Large maps are the most difficult to build on from a layout standpoint. It's not easy to get the traffic flow right, even if you stick to all the basic zoo-design principles! The grid layout doesn't work so well on large maps, at least not after you've begun expanding into the zoo's rear half; it's difficult to ensure every part of your zoo gets its share of guests. The High Street approach doesn't work well, either, because the distance between the center and the side walls is just too great. You need at least two big guest service areas, and preferably three or even four smaller ones. If placing two, create two short High Streets running parallel to the front and back zoo walls. If placing three, follow the advice for the medium map, noting that all three guest service areas will be slightly bigger. If placing four guest service areas, locate each small-to-medium-size block of guest amenities and amusements near a corner of the zoo. You don't want to tuck them into corners! The space next to the zoo wall should always be taken up by an exhibit (one corner of your zoo will be occupied by a compost building).

You'll find more details on placing guest service areas, guest amenities, and zoo decor in Chapter 3.

MODIFYING TERRAIN

You can set about building your zoo using one of two approaches. First, you can choose to keep terrain features intact as much as possible, which is a good choice if you're playing a relaxed game and intend to spend a lot of time strolling around and enjoying the scenery in your zoo. The second approach, recommended for goal-oriented games, is to flatten everything before beginning construction. You can easily add hills and valleys later, when you're done with building.

Don't hesitate to use low chain-link fence as scaffolding! It costs only $10 a section (purchase price minus recycling price). The effect of each terrain-modifying tool stops at the fence. This lets you build elevated pathways and moats with nice, neat edges. If you want the chosen tool to ignore the fence and pass under it, press and hold the Shift key together with the left mouse button.

Using the terrain-modifying tools in *ZT2* requires a bit of practice. Here are a few points about the individual terrain tools to help you get started quickly:

NOTE

ZT2 makes adding and modeling terrain features extremely easy, and all terrain alterations are free of charge. You're never stuck with any type of terrain.

🐾 **Create Hill.** You'll be using this tool for one purpose only: to create hills. Move the brush while holding down the left mouse button to create a ridge—very useful when trying to ensure privacy for an animal that does not use a man-made shelter. Work the hills over with the Smooth Terrain tool (see page 25) to finish them off.

🐾 **Create Valley.** This tool is used to create dips and valleys, as well as sunken exhibits. To create a sunken exhibit, fence off the exhibit area, then create a valley in the center, making it as deep as the future exhibit floor. Then use the Flatten Terrain tool (discussed on page 25) to sink the entire exhibit floor (see Figure 2.3)

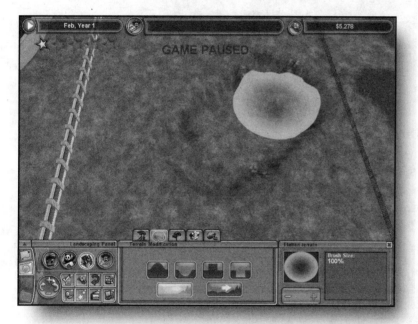

FIGURE 2.3:
Sink the exhibit floor with the Flatten Terrain tool by stroking outward from the center valley.

🐾 **Create Cliff.** This tool is used to create cliffs and elevated pathways. To create an elevated pathway, raise a cliff to the desired height, then stretch it with the Flatten Terrain tool, brushing from the cliff top and along the route of the elevated pathway. If you want your elevated pathway to have nice, neat edges, use low chain-link fence for scaffolding (see Figure 2.4).

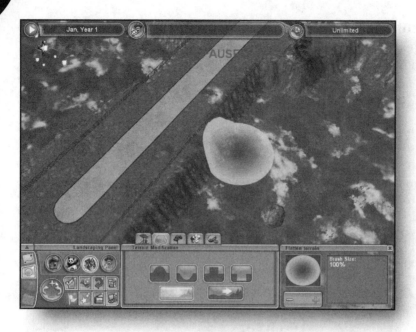

FIGURE 2.4:
Use cheap fence scaffolding to shape elevated pathways.

Create Ditch. This tool is used exclusively to create moats, which can be employed as exhibit barriers in *ZT2*; they are not very economical in terms of space, so they are an option that's best reserved for larger maps. Creating a moat without using fencing for scaffolding can turn into a horror story; mark out the proposed moat with low chain-link fence before using the Create Ditch tool (see Figure 2.5).

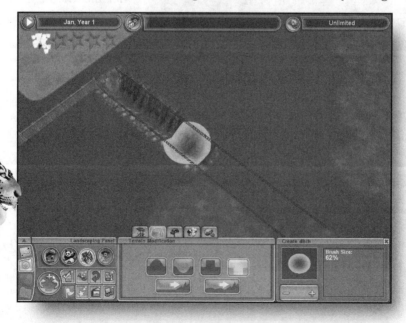

FIGURE 2.5:
This is the easiest way to dig a moat.

Flatten Terrain. This is a very important tool that truly makes modifying terrain a snap: a dangerous-looking mountain range can be erased in seconds! You'll use this tool extensively, either flattening the whole zoo area to start with, or flattening terrain selectively for pathways, exhibits, guest service areas, etc. As mentioned earlier, the Flatten Terrain tool is also used to create elevated pathways and sunken exhibits. Just click on the spot that has the elevation you want, then drag the mouse to bring terrain to that elevation, filling in ditches and valleys and flattening hills.

Smooth Terrain. This tool plays a very important role in the game. Using it softens terrain features, making them accessible by people and animals. It's indispensable when building paths and fences in hilly terrain. Inaccessible terrain is shaded yellow; passing the Smooth Terrain tool over the affected area removes the yellow and the problem. Most importantly, you'll use the Smooth Terrain brush to enable your zookeepers to access sunken exhibits (see Figure 2.6).

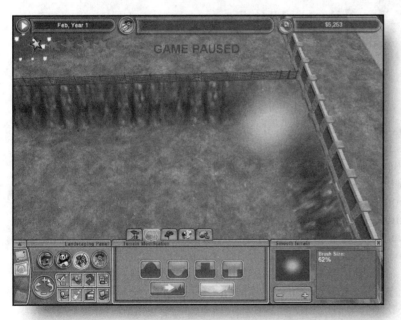

FIGURE 2.6:
Use the Smooth Terrain tool to create sunken-exhibit access ramps for zookeepers.

BUILDING EXHIBITS

You can create exhibits in three different ways in *Zoo Tycoon 2*. Here are your choices:

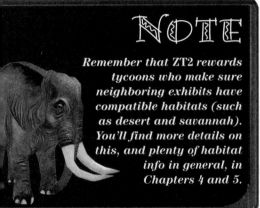

🐾 **Classic exhibit.** You simply fence off an area using the fence-placement mode of your choice (rubber band, rectangular, octagonal). This is the simplest way to build an exhibit.

🐾 **Sunken exhibit.** After fencing off the exhibit area, you sink the exhibit floor. If you sink it far enough for cliffs to appear along the fence, the animals are automatically contained by the cliff barrier (you'll still need a fence of some sort to keep guests from falling in). You may also sink it to a smaller depth and use a fence as an extra barrier—see the Fencing Notes section on the following page.

🐾 **Moat exhibit.** The moat acts as the exhibit barrier, but you'll still need fencing, decorative or standard, so that the guests don't fall in. Exhibits with moats take up a lot of space and, predictably, aren't easy to expand. You pay an extra price for the stunning appearance!

You may also create sunken exhibits by raising the pathways and guest areas instead of sinking the exhibit floor (as demonstrated in the Biome Squares map in the game). This is a very spectacular solution, but it does have a significant drawback. As your zoo grows, something as simple as adding an unplanned restroom may force you to expand the elevated area, thus reducing the size of the neighboring exhibits. This goes against the general need to *expand* exhibits as the game goes on, and may create all sorts of problems, particularly if your animals have been breeding vigorously.

All in all, the sunken exhibit is the happiest choice, for several reasons. Expanding it isn't more difficult than expanding a classic fenced exhibit; a few swipes with the Flatten Terrain tool, and you're done. The difference in elevation gives a better view of animals, making guests happier. Finally, sinking the exhibit floor means you can use cheaper low fencing to contain it. As mentioned earlier, you always need a fence to keep guests from falling in; so you might as well sink the exhibit floor to a smaller depth and use low exhibit fencing to complete the barrier (see Figure 2.7).

FIGURE 2.7:
Low fencing and sunken exhibits cost little and give guests great views of the animals.

The big rule to keep in mind when building an exhibit is this: always make it bigger than you think necessary to start with, and leave some room for future expansion. The no-charge terrain tools and biome brushes make ongoing exhibit evolution a very good tactic when playing the game.

FENCING NOTES

There are two main types of fencing in *ZT2*: exhibit fencing and decorative fencing. Exhibit fencing is used primarily to contain animals; decorative fencing is used to contain guests; i.e., to keep them where you want them. Decorative fencing is appreciated by adult guests, while exhibit fencing has a strength value: the higher the strength value, the stronger the animals it can contain without danger of their breaking out.

The big thing about *ZT2*, however, is that *happy animals do not break out*. Why would they want to, if they are happy? What's more, the game's number-one goal is to keep animals happy. You won't have a problem with that—you've got this guide, after all. So there are really only two types of exhibit fencing you ever need to use. One is high wooden slat fencing (available at one-star fame) that you will use to provide privacy for your animals. The other is cheap, low chain-link fencing. You'll use it for scaffolding as explained earlier, and you'll employ it to top off your sunken exhibits if the elevation difference isn't an effective barrier in itself (no cliffs). If you've sunk the exhibit deep enough for cliffs to form, you might as well use a decorative fence to please the guests that little bit more.

NOTE

For more details on habitats and animal care, please refer to Chapters 4 and 5.

Naturally, you should feel free to use whatever fencing style you fancy most, as long as your zoo can afford it. But as far as practical benefits go, you don't need to. If you keep your animals happy, your zoo will be an Eden in which elephants show respect for matchstick fencing, and lions peacefully lie down with gazelles (in absence of lambs).

DETERMINING EXHIBIT SHAPE

ZT2 lets you build exhibits of any shape you'd like. However, some shapes are more practical than others. The two ready-made shapes available through fence-placement mode are rectangular and octagonal; the rectangular one is much more practical. An octagonal exhibit doesn't work well when it adjoins the zoo wall, or when it's very large; it's perfect for building small, single-species exhibits in high-traffic areas of your zoo, but only once you've researched solid fencing (see Figure 2.8). Expanding an octagonal exhibit is complicated, and most often means it ceases to be an octagonal exhibit.

FIGURE 2.8:

Use solid fencing to provide privacy for animals in octagonal exhibits.

The rectangular exhibit is much more flexible and adaptable. It is easy to plan and build; it's also easy to expand (see the Exhibit Evolution section). But all in all, the best course of action is to choose the rubber band fencing-placement mode, and give your exhibit the shape that best fits your plans.

Keep in mind that optimally, you want the exhibit to enclose the viewing area from three sides. This carries extra costs and may not be the way you'll build the exhibit initially, when playing a scenario or a Challenge game. However, it's something you should do once you can invest in exhibit improvement. The following section explains how to set about it.

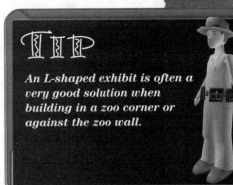

TIP

An L-shaped exhibit is often a very good solution when building in a zoo corner or against the zoo wall.

EXHIBIT EVOLUTION

Exhibit evolution is a phenomenon that occurs in Campaign scenarios and Challenge games. Freeform games let you build anything you like any time you like; you can pause the game and build a complete five-star zoo right at the start.

The economical exhibits you build at the beginning of a Challenge game or a Campaign scenario (see Figure 2.9) can be expanded and/or changed at minimal cost later on in the game. All you need to do is plan ahead and make sure the needed space is there. This dynamic approach to exhibit management is encouraged by free terrain tools and biome brushes. It costs little to transform an exhibit into a suitable home for a new species, or to create a three-sided viewing area for the zoo guests.

FIGURE 2.9:

Building this exhibit cost under $2,000.

This last move is especially important. Zoo guests can see much more if they can view the exhibit from multiple directions. The problem is, three-sided viewing areas cost a little more, and often require you to install solid high fencing that guides the guests into the viewing area and provides sufficient privacy for the animals. At the start of the game, there is no solid high fencing available. When wooden slat fencing becomes available at one-star fame, you'll most likely be too pressed for money to afford it: it's pricey at $110 a section, even given the recycling return on the replaced fencing, and a one-star-fame zoo has plenty of other, more pressing investments waiting to happen.

It makes sense to wait awhile before introducing three-sided viewing areas, and paying for the solid high fencing that guides the guests into the viewing area and provides the animals with privacy. You begin by building a simple sunken exhibit as shown in Figure 2.9. When funds and fencing options allow, you can transform the exhibit, creating a three-sided viewing area, as shown in Figure 2.10.

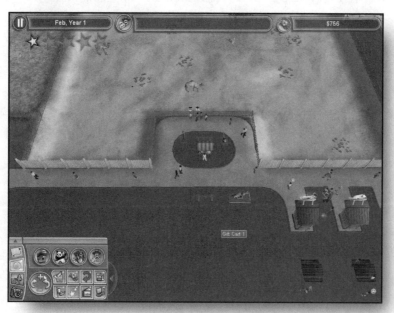

FIGURE 2.10:
Remodeling the cheap exhibit shown earlier costs under $2,000.

THE TYCOON AS ZOO MANAGER AND MR. MONEYBAGS

Once you've built your starting zoo, you have to run it and make sure it's profitable enough to finance its own expansion. Once again, these concerns do not apply if you're playing a Freeform game. They are crucial in all other games, however, especially in some of the Campaign scenarios. One of these, Scarce Asian Animals, will push your moneymaking and management skills to their limits, and you won't win it without being a dynamic tycoon, raking poop with one hand as you stuff dollars into your pocket with the other. The ability to multitask under trying conditions is the mark of an accomplished zoo manager. Let's take a closer look at what's involved.

RUNNING YOUR ZOO

Almost all Campaign scenarios and Challenge games will initially force you to roll up your sleeves and perform hands-on zoo-management duties. Most of these will involve caring for animals, which is covered in detail in Chapter 4. Trash is rarely a concern given the low number of guests. You will likely spend much of the first month of the game playing zookeeper, and briefly turn maintenance worker at the month's end.

When performing zookeeper duties, you shouldn't stop at checking on the animals' status through Quick Stats. One of the most important stats—the amount of poop in the exhibit—isn't

NOTE

Learn how to move around your zoo quickly! Jump to selected spots by using the Overview Map, or by clicking on the messages that appear on the message bar in the top center of the main game screen. Remember, you can also click on any animal, zoo employee, or guest on the Quick Stats panel to move to his or her location in the overhead view.

there. You'll hear about it only when it's out of control. The sharp-eyed tycoon can spot poop in the exhibit even from maximum zoom-out in the Overhead View; less-talented players should cruise at lower altitude, and use filters to clear foliage and other objects from view (open the filter panel by clicking on the arrowhead above the Map Overview button). If you can see poop out in the open, you can bet there will be more hidden from view: swoop down and

TIP

In the early game, you need to run through each of your exhibits just twice a month to ensure everything's in top shape. A peafowl exhibit may be an exception; like all birds, peafowl are pretty high-maintenance.

dispose of it instantly. Use the opportunity to deal with everything in this particular exhibit. The best way to do this is to run through the exhibit, responding to the requests for action that will arrive together with aural cues. Clean up all the poop (see Figure 2.11), groom all the animals that need grooming, refill all the food and water containers, and move on to repeat the same procedure in the next exhibit. Remember to place gates in convenient locations, and use the Shift key to run in first-person view.

FIGURE 2.11:

Feathered friends may seem like compost-making fiends when you're the harried zookeeper.

You'll turn maintenance worker only when clicking on a trash can reveals it's more than half-full. In a freshly started zoo, these duties take up so little time and effort they aren't worth discussing in detail. The only way you can get in trouble with trash is through gross negligence—not getting enough trash cans (at least two next to each other in dining areas), or letting trash accumulate while you're too busy with other things. You'll quickly be told there's a problem by the red, angry face emoticons over the guests' heads, and a scattering of trash on the pathways. Sweeping it up involves seconds, and limits the consequences to one or two guests leaving the zoo a little earlier.

Hiring and Managing Zoo Staff

It makes sense to hire zoo staff as soon as you have four or five exhibits (depending on the number and species of animals they contain). A zoo with that many exhibits makes enough money to let you keep expanding, in spite of the costs associated with hired help. The total cost of hiring a zookeeper and a maintenance worker is $700, which will be very affordable with four or five hardworking donation boxes; you'll be covering salary costs with income from zoo admissions and food, drink, and gift sales, leaving the donation money untouched.

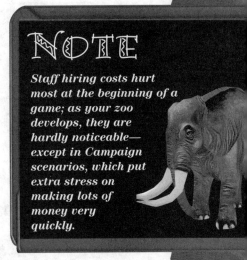

There are some general rules that you should remember when hiring and managing staff. The first rule is that the number of needed zookeepers grows much faster than the number of exhibits in your zoo. At first, one zookeeper can handle four starting exhibits; late in the game, you might need *two* zookeepers assigned to just one big multispecies exhibit. The number of zookeepers you need varies greatly depending on whether you're breeding animals in your zoo, as well as the species you have. These details are covered in Chapters 4 and 5.

The second general rule is that you never need more than three maintenance workers—not even in the largest zoos. In most games, two maintenance workers will be more than enough, and you can certainly build and maintain a five-star zoo using just one. Maintenance worker costs are insignificant, and management problems nonexistent. They are wonderfully efficient in comparison with the golden-hatted wonders in the original *Zoo Tycoon*.

The third general rule of staff management is that you should begin hiring educators as soon as you have more than 60 guests in your zoo (see Figure 2.12). Educators are not expensive at $200 a month (although there is the one-time expense of $500 for the educator podium), and they'll make you money through increased donations if there are enough guests doing the donating. You can add an extra educator for approximately every 20 guests after 60. You'll never need more than six educators, and in the vast majority of your games, you'll need just three or four—remember that you can move the educator's podium between various exhibits.

FIGURE 2.12:
Educators are great at attracting crowds and making guests happy to stuff more money into donation boxes.

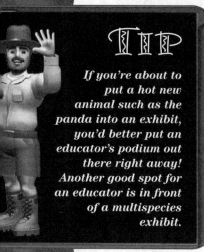

TIP

If you're about to put a hot new animal such as the panda into an exhibit, you'd better put an educator's podium out there right away! Another good spot for an educator is in front of a multispecies exhibit.

MAKING MONEY

Zoo Tycoon 2 features several sources of income for your zoo. The sources are the same as in the original *Zoo Tycoon*; however, their relative importance is vastly different. Veterans of the original game should take note!

One money source overshadows all others. This is the income you receive from guest donations. A five-star zoo earns around $30,000 a month in donations without any special effort such as micromanaging educators and fine-tuning guest amenities. Remember that in *ZT2*, guest amenities aren't as important for the money they can make directly as for the positive effect they have on guest happiness, and thus the size and frequency of guest donations.

ZOO INCOME

The manual discusses zoo income and expenditures in some detail. Here are a few extra observations on zoo income sources to help you get a better grip on your cash flow:

- **Guest donations** constitute roughly 75% of your zoo's total income in any month (give or take 10%, depending on other circumstances). Guests make donations when they like what they see in your exhibits. However, their overall happiness level is influenced by how well their needs are satisfied, so factors such as presence of guest amenities and amusements also play a role. Guest expectations play a part, too: charging admission to your zoo increases guest expectations. The higher the admission, the more a guest expects from your zoo; and if your zoo does not live up to these raised expectations, the disillusioned guest will donate less money to the zoo.

- **Admission** can account for 2–15% of your zoo's income. Admission can vary greatly depending on the price setting you've chosen, and what stage of the game you're in. Admission does not have an effect on the number of new guests in your zoo. However, as mentioned earlier, charging admission can negatively impact zoo donations. This might result in some misleading statistics: when you raise admission prices, admission money may grow in importance disproportionately because donations show a decrease. Giving guests free admission is a very viable strategy; the only time admission money truly counts is when you are starting your zoo from very humble beginnings (certain Campaign scenarios, low-starting-money Challenge games), and you're desperate for more dollars. Setting a Moderate-level admission to a one-star-fame zoo will make you around $600–700 a month, but if your animals aren't really happy, you might see a decrease in donations.

> **TIP**
>
> *Sticking to the default Moderate admission price is a safe move through most of the game. It results in a handy trickle of dollars without greatly affecting guests' expectations. Setting admission to High may result in smaller guest donations unless you run a truly world-class zoo. Low admission is a safe choice for a half-star zoo with four exhibits.*

- **Food and drink sales** bring in roughly 5–10% of your income, depending on the stage of your zoo development and the prices you charge. Remember, you can provide drinks and food for free if that's your fancy; predictably, it will make zoo guests happy. However, they'll also be happy if you charge reasonable prices and provide them with a place to sit down while they are eating and drinking—Chapter 3 has more details.

✂ **Gift sales** bring in approximately another 5–10% of your zoo's income, again depending on the prices you charge. This income is labeled Shop Sales in the game's financial report, but includes income from both gift carts and gift shops.

✂ **Recycling** can contribute as much as 10% of your zoo's income *if* you've built a compost building; recycling bins provide only a trickle of small change. Recycling income includes the money you get for removed zoo objects, so you will see sudden spikes whenever you go on a rampage with the bulldozer. Recycling income is particularly important in games that involve a tight budget (see Figure 2.13).

FIGURE 2.13:

That little building may net you as much money as all the food and drink stands in your zoo.

✂ **Cash grants** vary in importance between games. They're quite important in Challenge games; the grants you get upon completing challenges are vital to the quick development of your zoo. In the Campaign game, cash grants are featured only in selected scenarios (for example, Animal Adoption Programs or African Animal Empire). They're helpful, but not as vital as they are in Challenge games. Note that the starting money you receive is listed as a cash grant.

Maximizing zoo income in *ZT2* is a very straightforward process. You must make your animals as happy as possible, with guest happiness coming second (it will be boosted automatically by the happy animals). All the other maneuvers you can make, such as hiking admission/food and drink stand/gift prices, have minimal effect in comparison with the donation money tap that opens when your animals are truly happy.

Zoo Expenditures

Zoo expenditures are also discussed in the game manual. They're pretty self-explanatory, but here are a few extra comments:

- **Animal adoption** costs are unavoidable expenses that grow sharply as the game goes on. Adopting a pair of camels at the start costs $2,500; adopting a pair of giant pandas, $100,000. The only way you can keep adoption costs down is by breeding animals in your zoo so that you never need replacements for animals that die (hopefully of old age). However, breeding animals sharply increases upkeep costs, and possibly zoo payroll (extra zookeepers), so there's no way you can actually save money in this area. Animal adoption is more expensive than anything else in the game. You'll often find yourself staring at the money counter while saving up for an exotic species.

- **Animal upkeep** is a major expense throughout the game. It varies depending on how many new food and drink containers you've bought in a given month; upkeep costs may double if you and your zookeepers were particularly busy replenishing animal food supplies. The animal upkeep costs in a big five-star zoo can touch $5,000 monthly, even when you don't buy any new food or water containers.

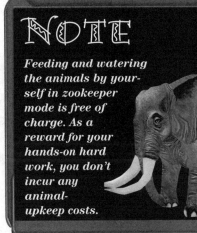

NOTE

Feeding and watering the animals by yourself in zookeeper mode is free of charge. As a reward for your hands-on hard work, you don't incur any animal-upkeep costs.

- **Construction** costs are, predictably, very heavy at the start of a game. Early on, it costs more to build and connect an exhibit than to adopt a pair of animals. By the middle game, exhibit costs—actually, any building costs—will seem small in comparison with adoption costs. You can minimize construction costs by opting for sunken exhibits and low, cheap fencing. You can also economize, to some extent, by planning your zoo very carefully—a perfectly placed restroom saves you from building two. Construction costs escalate sharply if you go for zoo decor in a big way. However, if you do well in other areas important to guest happiness, zoo decor becomes less important. See Chapter 3 for more details.

- **Staff salaries** rise steadily throughout the game. At the start of a Campaign scenario or low-starting-money Challenge game, you'll be doing everything yourself, so staff cost will equal zero. By the time your zoo hits five-star status, monthly staff costs are likely to be around $5,000 (an adequate number of zookeepers, a couple of maintenance workers, a couple of educators). A big zoo will have you busy helping out zookeepers no matter how many you hire!

- **Research** costs can vary wildly—there will be many months in which you won't do any research, and there will be months (especially after a fame increase) in which you will spend $5,000 or more. Increasing zoo fame by a full star always opens up numerous new research options. As mentioned elsewhere in this guide, you should never research something you don't intend to acquire in the very near future. If you manage to stick to this rule, monthly research costs will likely never exceed $2,000.

- **Upkeep** costs are maintenance costs associated with zoo buildings, such as food and drink stands. They are minimal at the start of the game, and climb slowly to touch $1,000 a month around the time your zoo acquires four-star fame. They tend to stay under $1,500 a month, even in big five-star zoos. You can minimize upkeep costs by placing every building in the right spot, and building only what has to be built; but upkeep will make only a minimal difference in overall zoo expenditures.

In summary, most zoo expenditures are unavoidable, and trying to minimize them isn't worth the effort *except* when building an exhibit. The expense of adopting a new species can be met sooner if you manage to save a couple of thousand dollars on fencing!

Now that you know all that there's to know about getting rich, let's talk about fame.

THE BENEFITS OF FAME

NOTE

Appendix B contains a full list of buildings, structures, and objects unlocked by higher fame levels, with research costs where applicable.

The concept of zoo fame and what goes into it is explained in the game manual and reviewed in Chapter 1 of this guide. Here, let's look at the practical benefits of fame.

The number-one practical benefit is that higher fame gives you adoption rights to new species, and opens up extra adoption slots—from three at half-star fame to the maximum nine at four stars. Each half-star advance in fame is rewarded by adoption rights to several new species, while each full-star advance gets you one extra adoption slot (one- and two-star fame) or two extra adoption slots (three- and four-star fame).

Increasing your zoo's fame by a full star also makes available many new zoo structures and objects (see Figure 2.14). These include guest service buildings, zoo decor, animal enrichment objects, new types of animal shelters, and new varieties of vegetation and rocks. Vegetation and rocks never need to be researched, but many of the other objects and structures do. Animal enrichment objects and shelters are frequently expensive to research and place! For example, equipping a peafowl exhibit with an enrichment object and a shelter will cost you more than adopting a pair of these birds.

FIGURE 2.14:

No more bathroom lines! Two-star fame brings a revolution in guest amenities: the family restroom.

Every full-star advance in fame is an important milestone in the development of your zoo. Note that it is possible to build a five-star zoo without doing any research at all. Solid fencing can be made unnecessary by screens of trees and terrain features, and the guest service structures that require research do not absolutely need to be built. You can max out guest happiness without them by doing what is recommended repeatedly throughout this guide: concentrate on the happiness of your animals. Although acquiring new animal toys through research helps make your animals happy, you can make animals happy enough without them. Chapters 4 and 5 have all the relevant details.

Higher fame also lets you max out admission prices, but as discussed earlier, that may have an adverse affect on donations. The successful tycoon strives to increase money from donations since they are the lifeblood of your zoo. Guest donations and guest happiness in general are the subject of the next chapter.

TIP

Completing the Campaign game unlocks several zoo-decor objects that can be used in any game right from its start. This makes it easier to reach five-star fame without any research.

CHAPTER 3

MAKING PEOPLE HAPPY

WHAT MAKES PEOPLE HAPPY? IN *ZOO TYCOON 2*, THE ANSWER TO THAT QUESTION IS MERCI-FULLY EASY—EASY ENOUGH TO BE CONTAINED WITHIN THIS CHAPTER, WHICH DISCUSSES ZOO GUESTS. YOU WILL LEARN WHO YOUR GUESTS ARE, WHY THEY COME TO YOUR ZOO, AND WHAT MOTIVATES THEM ONCE THEY PASS THROUGH YOUR FRONT GATES. YOU'LL ALSO FIND OUT HOW MUCH MONEY THEY BRING WITH THEM, AND HOW THEY'RE INCLINED TO SPEND IT.

A LARGE PART OF THIS CHAPTER FOCUSES ON FACTORS THAT AFFECT GUEST HAPPINESS. YOU KNOW BY NOW THAT ANIMAL HAPPINESS IS THE LARGEST SINGLE FACTOR; HOWEVER, YOU ALSO KNOW FROM THE GAME AND THE MANUAL THAT GUESTS HAVE NEEDS, JUST LIKE YOUR ANIMALS. IF THESE NEEDS REMAIN UNSATISFIED, GUESTS WILL ANGRILY LEAVE YOUR ZOO REGARDLESS OF THE JOY THAT REIGNS SUPREME IN ALL YOUR EXHIBITS. THIS CHAPTER EXPLAINS HOW TO GIVE GUESTS WHAT THEY NEED SO THAT THEY RECIPROCATE BY GIVING YOU WHAT *YOU* NEED: PLENTY OF MONEY.

BE SURE TO READ THE TOP 10 TIPS FOR ATTRACTING GUESTS TO YOUR ZOO ON PAGE 10 OF YOUR GAME MANUAL. THEY AREN'T REPEATED HERE.

WHO THEY ARE

The world of *Zoo Tycoon 2* is a fair, balanced world: 50% of the guests that come to your zoo are adults, and 50% are children. You should see these proportions reflected when you click around on the people in your zoo. If you don't, it may be that the needs of one group are not being met, causing guests in that group to leave your zoo early! Later in this chapter, you'll learn how to prevent that from occurring.

The guests that enter your zoo always have plenty of money on them: between $400 and $600. Adult guests can replenish their money supply by hitting the ATM (they'll withdraw a random sum between $400 and $600), but child guests can't—their cash is limited to what's in their pockets when they enter the zoo. However, it's likely it will last longer: children's donations are 50% smaller than adults' donations. Of course, children also pay half-price admission to your zoo: if you set it at Moderate or $20, a child guest will pay $10.

Every guest that enters your zoo has a favorite animal. The species of that animal depends on the reasons that made the guest visit your zoo. Most of your guests come because they've heard about your zoo; they know something about it already. The favorite animal species of most of these guests is thus randomly chosen from the adoption pool available to you at your zoo's fame level. This favorite species is switched for another after a while in a gradual, seamless manner.

FIGURE 3.1:

So you'd like to see a tiger, eh? Stick around, donate plenty of money, and we'll see.

However, not all of your guests come with a clear intent; you'll also get guests who just happened to drop into your zoo on a caprice. The favorite species of these happy-go-lucky guests are randomly selected from all the species in the game. Fortunately, these clueless guests are a distinct minority (see Figure 3.1).

Note that it's not possible to guarantee guests will get to see their favorite animals. Adopting all the species available at your fame level almost immediately raises fame level, which in turn gives you adoption rights to more animals; you'll never catch up for long. However, you have a better chance of exhibiting many guests' favorite animals if you display as many species as you can.

NOTE

A zoo guest doubles the donation amount upon seeing a favorite animal.

WHAT MOVES THEM

Guests are moved by their needs. The need that motivates them to enter your zoo is, of course, the desire to see your animals. In addition to that, guests have six needs that are shown on the guest-info panel.

To begin with, all zoo guests have one overwhelming need: they want to be happy. In addition, each guest has five basic needs. All guest needs and their levels of satisfaction are shown on the guest-info panel:

- **Happiness.** This isn't a need in itself; happiness is a yardstick for measuring how much a zoo guest likes your zoo. Satisfying any of the five basic needs carries a happiness bonus, as well. Big happiness boosts come from being able to obtain favorite food and drink, and consuming them while comfortably seated.

- **Hunger.** Guests like to be fed just as much as your animals do. What's more, they are willing to pay for it. Guests have different food preferences; for easy reference, these are listed in Appendix B. For now, note that it's easier to cater to children: they are much less demanding than adults.

- **Thirst.** Guests will pay good money to slake their thirst. Adults and children have different drink preferences.

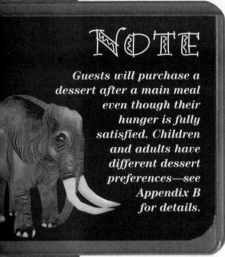

- **Rest.** When guests get tired, they like to sit down and have a rest. They rest best in gazebos; umbrella and picnic tables come second; and benches are a somewhat distant third. Note, however, that guests who aren't consuming food or a drink use only benches.

- **Amusement.** Guests desire to be entertained not only by the animals, but also by the zoo itself. Adults and children have different amusement preferences. Children like bouncy rides, playgrounds, and Shetland pony rides; adults are entertained by looking at zoo decor (see Figure 3.2). Everyone loves the animal kiosks—insect house and reptile house.

- **Bathroom.** This important need is satisfied in restrooms. Predictably, it grows sharply after a guest has consumed something in your zoo.

FIGURE 3.2:
The flower arch guarantees a shot of happiness to every adult guest that looks at it.

Guests tend to satisfy their needs, starting with the need that's easiest to satisfy. A somewhat hungry guest who needs to visit the restroom really badly might choose to eat first if the restroom's farther away than a food stand.

The typical sequence of guest actions when they enter the zoo is to go to the most attractive exhibit in the vicinity of the entrance. The more time they spend there, the higher their basic needs by the time they're done. However, before satisfying basic needs, guests react to what they saw in the exhibit. If they liked what they saw, they'll give your zoo a donation; then they'll purchase souvenirs from a gift cart—as long as basic needs haven't become pressing. By the time that cycle is done, a guest is usually really ready to hit your guest service area to satisfy a basic need or two.

Remember that multispecies exhibits drain guest cash very quickly! If an adult guest is truly impressed by the different species in your huge savannah exhibit, for example, the resulting repeated donations may almost equal all the cash the guest has brought into the zoo. If you needed yet another argument in favor of building multispecies exhibits, this is it! It is also an argument for placing an ATM near each exhibit that contains several species when you have 80 or more guests in your zoo.

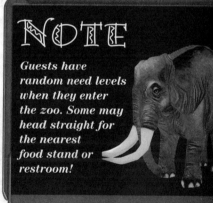

NOTE

Guests can and will buy multiple souvenirs if the exhibit they just viewed contained multiple species. For example, a guest that has just finished viewing a savannah exhibit might purchase both a stuffed gazelle and a stuffed giraffe from the gift cart.

How to Read Guest Needs

The guest-info panel features a row of need boxes that fill with color depending on the guest's need status. More color in the box is bad; less is good. Here's what each box color represents:

NOTE

Guests have random need levels when they enter the zoo. Some may head straight for the nearest food stand or restroom!

- **Transparent (fully satisfied)**—guest need is 70% to 100% satisfied.

- **Green (satisfied)**—guest need is 30% to 70% satisfied.

- **Yellow (pressing)**—guest need is 10% to 30% satisfied.

- **Red (critical)**—a need satisfaction level below 10% means a guest need isn't satisfied.

When a guest need is critical and isn't being satisfied, the guest's happiness begins dropping. A guest that isn't happy any longer starts to think about leaving the zoo. If enough time passes (a couple of real-time minutes) without the guest being able to meet the critical need, the guest leaves the zoo without viewing any more exhibits, and without stuffing more money into your donation boxes. However, if all of a guest's needs are satisfied, the guest will continue touring your zoo until he's seen all of its exhibits.

What They See

A guest entering your zoo is aware of all the animals you have on display without actually seeing them. Therefore, a guest can choose to go to a specific exhibit even though it's far away and out of sight.

Zoo guests see things differently depending on what they're looking at: animals inside exhibits, or zoo buildings and objects.

- **Guests have an animal-viewing range** of just over 9.5 tiles without binoculars, and approximately 21 tiles with binoculars when looking at animals inside an exhibit. Note that binoculars have to be within 10 tiles of the exhibit to be usable, and that a path or paved area has to be within three tiles of the exhibit to act as a viewing area. Remember that guests standing in a three-sided viewing area can view a much larger exhibit area—they can look to the front *and* to the sides. Refer to the Exhibit Evolution section of Chapter 2 for more details.

- **Guests have a building-spotting range** of up to 16 tiles for big build-ings, such as a restaurant (see Figure 3.3). However, smaller buildings such as food and drink stands can be seen only at ranges of up to 13 tiles , and smaller objects such as trash cans must be even closer (within seven tiles). Note that adult guests have to stand within three tiles of a zoo-decor object before they even decide whether they'll look at it and gain its amusement and happiness bonuses.

FIGURE 3.3:
Aha! A place to sit down and eat.

Guests decide where they'll stand to view an animal based on two factors: the viewable area of the exhibit, and closeness of the exhibit. In short, guests want to see as much as possible, as close up as possible. But if standing closer to the exhibit means getting a worse view, they'll move back.

You can make sure guests always stand where they're supposed to by making the view from the viewing area better than the views from anyplace else. Simply arrange the features inside the exhibit with the guests' view in mind, using common sense: don't plant trees, raise hills, or otherwise block the view with an object right in front of the viewing area.

If you plan your exhibit around the advice in this guide, every viewing area will offer guests a great view. As explained in Chapter 4, you'll be marking out a food-serving area in all of your exhibits right in front of the viewing area. This ensures guests will get to see the animals from up close, because animals have to eat and drink. The animals' food-serving area has to have plenty of open space so that both the animals and the zookeepers can easily get to the food and drink. Open space ensures that guests get a great view of the exhibit.

WATCHING THE ANIMALf

Guests come to your zoo to see interesting animals in interesting settings. They want to see beautifully modeled biomes that will provide educational benefit, they want to see entertaining animal behavior, and they want to see baby animals! Every tycoon playing on a larger map should have at least a dozen species blissfully breeding in the zoo.

TIP

Providing an animal with its favorite type of shelter quickly pays for itself. As you will see, guests can also get a kick out of watching an animal sleep!

It's been said before, but here it is again so that you'll *always* remember it: guests like to watch animals from three-sided viewing areas that adjoin the exhibit and are equipped with binoculars. Every viewing area like that should have two donation boxes—they'll be busy. Letting your guests see more means you'll see more money coming in.

Guests get an educational benefit from an exhibit if it faithfully re-creates the animals' natural environment (see Chapter 4). You can tell when a guest has had an educational experience by the special educational smiley that appears over the guest's head, and by monitoring guest thoughts on the guest-info panel. Thoughts that indicate educational benefits appear in white type.

Thoughts that appear in green type indicate the guest sees the animal as entertaining. Animals are judged as entertaining when they engage in playful behavior such as chasing each other, taking dust baths, climbing trees, or using enrichment objects. Remember, these aren't limited to toys; they also include sophisticated devices such as the heated rock for savannah predators.

You increase educational benefits for the guests and raise animal happiness if you remember to zone exhibits correctly, so that closely neighboring biomes don't clash with each other (for example, tundra next to desert). Don't forget to read up on animal habitats and biome zoning in Chapter 4!

PLACING GUEST SERVICE BUILDINGS, STRUCTURES, AND ZOO DECOR

Zoo guests' viewing and spotting ranges provide a hint on optimal spacing between zoo structures. Most guest amusements, such as bouncy rides, fountains, and sundials, can be spotted only from a range of 6.5 tiles or less, and a guest shouldn't walk more than half a dozen tiles before spotting a new amusement. This translates into placing guest amusements every 20 tiles or so. Use a similar template when placing guest service areas. A zoo guest shouldn't have to walk more than 25 tiles before spotting the buildings; that gives you a maximum inter-area distance of 60 tiles. Of course, you should place extra restrooms and benches, as well as gift carts and rides for the children. A bench and a gift cart should be placed next to every exhibit-viewing area (see Figure 3.4); children's rides and restrooms should be placed every two to three exhibits.

FIGURE 3.4:

Give zoo guests a chance to rest and buy a gift when they've finished visiting an exhibit.

You should also be thoughtful about how you place buildings and structures inside a guest service area. A guest should spend a minimal amount of time going from one building to another. There are many such trips, because guests purchase and consume one item at a time! Guest movements follow a predictable pattern: a food or drink purchase is followed by a trip to the best seating available within guest spotting range; consumption while sitting down is followed by a trip to the trash can. Consumption of both food and drink often means a subsequent trip to the restroom. You should arrange your guest service area accordingly. Include amusements within its perimeter to cater to that need as well; you'll probably add some decor automatically, but don't forget playgrounds for the children. These take up more space than the bouncy rides, and thus fit in better as part of a guest service area.

The two biggest winners, amusement-wise, are the insect and reptile houses (see Figure 3.5). A visit to either completely satisfies the amusement needs of all zoo guests. Don't be afraid to build multiple insect and reptile houses on larger maps! Each guest service area should have one; they are small and fit in easily.

NOTE

Guests whose needs are less than 50% satisfied won't buy gifts.

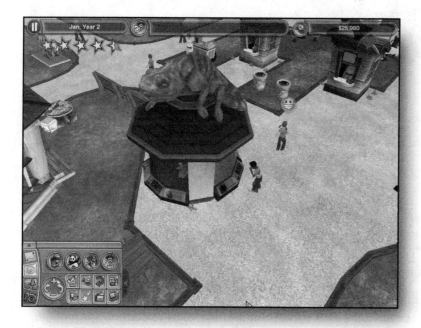

FIGURE 3.5:

All zoo guests love the insect and reptile houses.

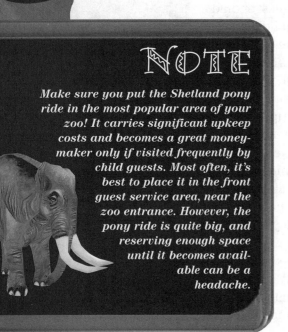

Always strive to plan your guest areas for efficient guest movement, because your ultimate aim is to make the guest's stay in your zoo more efficient, or *shorter*. This is in strong contrast to the original *Zoo Tycoon*, in which the aim was to trap the guest in a web of exhibits and concessions. Remember: a zoo guest with satisfied needs will tour your zoo until he's visited all exhibits. The quicker your guests see all the exhibits and leave, the quicker new guests will be spawned. New guests are basically walking wallets with $400 to $600 apiece. They'll leave all that and more in your zoo. Squeezing a handful of extra food and drink sales out of a touring guest is counterproductive; you'll make a few bucks, but also postpone the arrival of a new wallet filled to bursting with dollars ready to find their way into your donation boxes.

FOOD AND DRINK

The three types of zoo guests in *ZT2* (children, adult males, and adult females) have their own food and drink preferences. Supplying a zoo guest with favorite food and drink provides a greater happiness boost. Forcing a zoo guest to consume non-favorite food and drink at high prices causes a happiness drop! Here's who likes what:

- **Children** like burgers, hot dogs, cotton candy, ice cream, and soda. As you can see, it's quite fortunate that children constitute 50% of the zoo guests, because their food and drink preferences can be met early in the game in spite of your zoo's low fame.

- **Adult males** like shishkebabs, subs, cheesecake, popcorn, water, and coffee. None of these choices are available at the start of a Challenge game or Campaign scenario, and only the popcorn cart is available at one-star fame. Poor guys just have to wait!

- **Adult females** like salads, sushi, fruit cups, pretzels, water, and coffee. A pretzel cart is available right at the start at half-star fame, but you'll have to wait awhile before you can acquire the other choices for your zoo.

Given this knowledge, you shouldn't have a problem setting research priorities when new buildings become available. Remember that only approximately 25% of the zoo guests are adult males, and 25% are adult females; children are the most populous group of zoo consumers. When you get around to building your second guest service center, researching a family restaurant and placing it instead of stands that sell children's favorites is always a very profitable move.

NOTE

A family restaurant caters to children, a restaurant caters to adult females, and a fancy restaurant caters to adult males.

You can set food, drink, and gift prices at three different levels: Low, Moderate, and High. In theory, you can afford to begin price-gouging zoo guests when everyone can get their favorite food; buying a favorite food or drink at a high price does not cause a drop in guest happiness. Here's how prices and food/drink availability influence zoo guests' moods:

- **Low prices:** all guests get a boost in happiness, including guests forced to consume non-favorite food and drink. The happiness boost is twice as big if the food/drink is a favorite.

- **Moderate prices:** guests who purchase a favorite food or drink get a boost in happiness. Guests who purchase a non-favorite item are neutral.

- **High prices:** guests who purchase a favorite food or drink are neutral. Guests who purchase a non-favorite item suffer a drop in happiness.

In practice, it's safest to keep food, drink, and gift prices at the default Moderate level (see Figure 3.6). Moderate prices ensure a meaningful profit without anyone's happiness getting hit. Once your zoo grows to four-star fame, you can consider jacking the prices up to High even though this will result in happiness hits. A four-star zoo easily keeps guests 100% happy in spite of the happiness hits incurred while paying high prices for non-favorite items.

Moderate prices mean nice profits and plenty of smiling faces.

TIP

Review food- and drink-stand profits if you build a restaurant nearby! A restaurant can wipe out the profits of stands and carts if it happens to offer the same food, drink, and dessert items. Remember that the three different types of restaurants sell different food, drink, and dessert combinations, and a fancy restaurant may work well where a family restaurant won't.

CARING FOR ANIMALS

THE WORLD OF *ZOO TYCOON 2* REVOLVES AROUND ANIMALS. THEY'RE THE REASON YOUR ZOO EXISTS, AND MAKING THEM HAPPY IS YOUR PRIMARY GOAL IN EVERY GAME.

THIS CHAPTER DISCUSSES EVERYTHING THAT MAKES ANIMALS HAPPY. FOR EASE OF REFERENCE, ANIMAL HAPPINESS IS DISCUSSED NEED BY NEED IN THE ORDER THE NEEDS APPEAR ON THE ANIMAL-INFO PANEL. YOU'LL LEARN WHAT AFFECTS EVERY ANIMAL NEED (BOTH POSITIVE AND NEGATIVE), AND WHAT TO DO TO KEEP YOUR ANIMALS TOTALLY SATISFIED. AS YOU'LL FIND OUT, KEEPING ANIMALS COMPLETELY HAPPY INVOLVES MANY VERY DIFFERENT FACTORS. ANIMAL CARE STARTS WITH EXHIBIT DESIGN AND ZONING, AND INVOLVES RE-CREATING THE ANIMAL'S NATURAL HABITAT. EVEN THE MOST ATTENTIVE ZOOKEEPER IN THE WORLD WILL BE UNABLE TO SATISFY SOME ANIMAL NEEDS IF CERTAIN CONDITIONS AREN'T FULFILLED.

PLEASE NOTE THAT CHAPTER 5 DISCUSSES ASPECTS OF ANIMAL CARE FOR INDIVIDUAL SPECIES. APPENDIX A CONTAINS IMPORTANT ANIMAL DATA FOR EASY REFERENCE.

WHAT THEY NEED

Every animal has a total of nine needs: five basic, and four advanced. Not meeting a basic need has graver consequences than not meeting an advanced need. Animals become angry and try to escape only when basic needs aren't met. But *Zoo Tycoon 2* isn't about keeping animals captive. It's about making them as happy as (or even happier than) if they were free to roam. It's about making them think, "Free food and free service. Nice environment, too. Hmmm, looks like a good place to start a family."

Note that the need boxes on the animal-info panel work exactly the same as the guest-need boxes discussed in Chapter 3. A clear box is very good news; green is good; yellow is alarming; red is bad. You won't be able to prevent a certain amount of green showing in most of the boxes, as animals have to feel a need before they try to satisfy it. However, you can and should keep the Environment need box completely clear, reacting quickly to any alarms (see Figure 4.1).

FIGURE 4.1:

Green alert! Color creeping into the Environment need box most likely means it's time to rake poop yet again.

The sections that follow discuss animal needs in the same order as they appear on the animal-info panel.

Satisfying Basic Animal Needs

The five basic animal needs are Biome, Hunger, Thirst, Rest, and Exercise. Holding the mouse cursor over a box will bring up a panel informing you of the need status. But of course, this isn't the only way to make sure none of these boxes are turning red!

There is a simple way to prevent this from ever occurring in your zoo. Check on the status of all your animals on the Quick Stats panel regularly. When one of the five basic animal needs reaches critical status and starts turning the need box red, it is only a matter of time before the animal concerned becomes angry; if it's not fed and watered, it can also fall ill. Treat a need box beginning to turn yellow as an alarm signal, and instantly click on the animal affected on the Quick Stats panel to jump to its location. Find out why its need is becoming pressing and what you can do to put things right. The sections below contain many solutions.

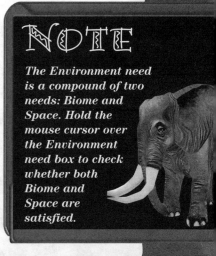

NOTE

The Environment need is a compound of two needs: Biome and Space. Hold the mouse cursor over the Environment need box to check whether both Biome and Space are satisfied.

NOTE

Overcrowding instantly changes the Environment need status to critical. You need to take immediate action! Overcrowded animals can't be released into the wild, but some can be temporarily crated. You can then consider putting some animals up for adoption—remember that all of their basic needs must be met before that's possible!

The Environment Need

The Environment need box indicates the animal's satisfaction with its habitat (Biome need), and the amount of space the animal has to itself (Space need). The space requirement varies from species and species and changes when adding extra animals of the species into the exhibit: the first animal requires much more space than the ones that follow. The relevant data is listed in Appendix A. Note that calculating an exhibit's area is easy if it's rectangular; things get murky with custom shapes.

Fully satisfying an animal's need for a suitable habitat is much more complex than counting off the necessary number of tiles. To begin with, you must create an appropriate habitat inside the exhibit. Here's how to set about it, taking care of a couple of other animal needs along the way:

TIP

Monitor the age of your older animals, and release them in time to retire in the wild, so to speak. Don't forget to raise replacements ahead of time! As a rule, you'll release your eldest animals into the wild and keep the younger ones until they age, too.

1. Make sure the exhibit is big enough to contain all the animals you intend to keep there in the future, then make it slightly bigger still. A good rule of thumb when adopting a pair is to plan the exhibit for six animals. If you try to stick to the most economical arrangement—a male and two females—you'll still have up to six animals in the exhibit at a time. They'll consist of the alpha male, two females, a couple of newborn animals, plus a juvenile male being raised to take over from the alpha male. Planning the exhibit for at least six animals from the start will let you avoid being surprised by unexpected pregnancies. Also, in addition to letting you mount a serious breeding operation, bigger exhibits don't get polluted with poop as quickly as smaller ones. You still have to get them clean, but not quite as often.

2. Model the terrain. If it's going to be an alpine habitat, create mountains and valleys. If it's going to be a savannah habitat, keep things relatively flat. To get an idea of what the terrain should look like, simply load a map of the given biome type from the Challenge or Freeform menu. Remember that terrain that's inaccessible to animals doesn't count toward meeting their Space needs. Don't go crazy with lakes and cliffs, and use the Smooth Terrain brush to ensure all slopes are accessible.

3. Paint the entire area inside the exhibit with a no-cost biome brush. Of course, the biome type should match the species you're going to put inside this exhibit.

4. Touch up the newly created habitat with other biome brushes from the selected biome palette (see Figure 4.2). Remember to add shallow or deep water as appropriate (see Appendix A for individual species' water preferences).

5. Add appropriate trees, plants, and rocks—if they're available. Some habitat items are available only after your zoo has reached a certain fame level; a lot of them are unlocked at two- and three-star zoo fame. The presence of trees, plants, and rocks that fit the habitat reinforces the animal's feeling that it is "at home," and provides an educational benefit for zoo guests.

FIGURE 4.2:

You don't need to make use of all biome brushes to meet a species' Biome need. However, it does make the biome look really nice.

6. Add an animal shelter if the species in question can use one, thus taking care of the animal's Privacy needs and letting it rest better. Numerous increasingly sophisticated animal shelters become available as your zoo grows in fame. Always build the highest-quality shelter that's available; if the species can use both a small wooden shelter and a rock cave, go with the rock cave. An animal sleeping in a high-quality shelter excites admiration among guests and stimulates the flow of dollars into donation boxes. Just think about that: while the animal is sleeping! Things don't get any better.

7. Place food and water for the animal(s) inside the exhibit. It's great if you can splurge for a variety of food, including the fancy variants if available (such as the rack of ribs for carnivores). This takes care of the hunger and the thirst. If you're counting pennies, you can place a little pond of shallow water instead of buying a water dish.

8. Place whatever enrichment objects you can get for the animal(s). This largely takes care of the Stimulation need. Many types of toys become available only at higher fame levels. Different enrichment objects provide the animal with different levels of stimulation. What's more, having many toys enables an animal to raise its stimulation level quickly. There's a mandatory delay before an animal can use the same object again.

4

NOTE

As a rule, the more you pay to acquire an animal need satisfier (shelter, toy, food container, or drink container), the more it will impress the guests when an animal uses it.

The easiest and quickest way to set up a habitat is to select the animal(s) you want on the adoption panel—you don't even have to adopt them. Then pause the game to click on the Zookeeper's Recommendations button on the animal-info panel. This puts everything you need to create a habitat for the chosen animal within a single mouse click. The number of options available—for example, types of trees or rocks—increases together with your zoo's fame. Appendix A lists the availability of habitat objects by fame level.

Remember that keeping the habitat clean is essential to maintaining its suitability. Animals don't like habitats strewn with poop, even if it's their own poop.

EXHIBIT ZONING

To create the best possible habitat for a given species, you must also zone it properly. The animals in the game are truly environment-sensitive: they are aware of the environment that exists outside their exhibit. If this outside environment clashes with the habitat inside the exhibit, complications ensue. The sensitive beasts inside the exhibit feel something is amiss. Looking at a tundra's icy expanse can be distressing to an okapi timidly peeking out from behind a banana tree in its tropical rainforest exhibit. Consult Appendix A to find the degree to which different habitats disagree with each other. The rule of thumb is that habitats that neighbor each other in the real world should neighbor each other in your zoo: alpine next to boreal forest, desert next to savannah, etc.

You *can* make a habitat fully acceptable to its inhabitants even when it clashes with a neighbor from which it is separated only by a shared fence. It involves placing as many trees, plants, and rocks as the species inside will tolerate—be careful, because an excess will lower the habitat's suitability. A camel won't like its desert turning into a date-palm forest! If you place the right amount of items, though, their combined presence reinforces the animal's sense of belonging, and weakens the effect of the clashing habitat in the neighboring exhibit. Nonetheless, the optimum habitat will have both good neighbors and the right number of trees, rocks, and plants (see Figure 4.3).

Painting a border around the exhibit with the appropriate biome brush improves the animals' perception of habitat quality.

THE HUNGER NEED

Satisfying animal hunger is very, very straightforward. You simply have to make sure it's always got enough food. If there's a variety of food available for a given species, get more than one kind. Place food containers near guest viewing areas; this will give zoo guests a chance to watch animals eat and also make it easier for zookeepers to replenish food supplies.

Occasionally, you may experience situations in which an animal goes hungry in spite of the fact that there's plenty of food in the exhibit. This usually occurs because it cannot get to the food for one of the following reasons:

🐾 While sculpting hills and valleys with the terrain tools, you made it impossible for an animal to get to where the food dishes are (they are always near either the guest viewing area or the zookeeper's gate). Work on your exhibit with the Smooth Terrain tool to soften steep slopes and blunt sharp edges.

🐾 While planting trees and placing rocks, you got a little carried away and didn't leave enough space for animals to pass through in a vital spot or two. Check the exhibit for impassable landslides and forests, and rearrange things as necessary.

🐾 The animal's path to the food is (temporarily) blocked by another animal.

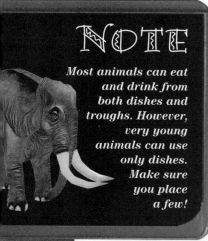
☝ All the dining seats are taken—there are too many hungry animals and too few food containers.

☝ Food and/or water containers have been placed too close to each other or to the fence. Larger animals, especially, need room to maneuver before taking a seat at the dinner table!

In all five cases, the immediate solution is to pick up the hungry animal and place it right next to the food, clearing a spot for it if necessary. You can also move the food or drink container, putting it in front of the needy animal. Then you should take whatever actions are necessary to prevent the problem from reoccurring: purchase more food containers, improve access to the food, move a few trees, and so on (see Figure 4.4).

FIGURE 4.4:
Turn each animal food-serving area into an easily accessible animal restaurant.

THE THIRST NEED

An animal's Thirst need is even less complicated than hunger: the only drink available is water. It's a good idea to have several water containers scattered around the exhibit in addition to the ones up front with the food; if you won't do it, most likely your zookeeper will. Don't forget about water dishes for young animals!

Animals can also drink water from ponds and lakes that you have created with a water brush. You must make sure that the shore allows animals easy access. Don't put ponds and lakes with deep water into exhibits with species that can't swim, and you'll save yourself plenty of aggravation (check Appendix A for species that swim).

Occasionally, an animal may be unable to get a drink for one of the reasons listed in the previous section. Follow the same emergency procedure.

THE REST NEED

Satisfying the Rest need rarely presents problems. There are only two situations in which an animal's Rest need may get critical. The first is when it is repeatedly trying to satisfy some other need and having no success. The second takes place when the tired animal continues to expend energy (by play-chasing, frolicking, wandering, running from a predator, or fighting a challenger male) in spite of a pressing Rest need. Animals rest in the shade, or in a shelter of an appropriate type. When you're working on the habitat, plant a few trees in a clump to provide a pool of deep shade—adding a dip in the ground will also give the resting animal some privacy. Some trees (for example, desert trees) don't provide a lot of shade, but when planted in groups always manage to do the job. If in doubt, purchase an umbrella shade!

THE EXERCISE NEED

You should not encounter any problems with animals meeting their need to exercise if you've faithfully re-created their natural environment and let them meet their other basic needs. Many species require deep water to get their necessary exercise (hippo, crocodile, polar bear, and others—please see Appendix A). Many animal actions, even simple wandering around, satisfy the need to exercise to some extent. However, the activity that satisfies it best is running (see Figure 4.5). In order to run, animals must have an obstacle-free course; make sure every habitat, even a heavily wooded forest, includes a clearing large enough for animals to run around! Since guests love to see animals running, it makes sense to place this clearing in front of the viewing area, where the food containers are. This will also make it easier for the animals to access the food, and for you to check on food supply by clicking on the container.

FIGURE 4.5:

Run, baby, run! Animals satisfy a range of needs when they play with each other.

NOTE

Chapter 5 and Appendix A have extra tips on satisfying the unique needs of individual species.

SATISFYING ADVANCED ANIMAL NEEDS

There are four advanced animal needs: Privacy, Hygiene, Social, and Stimulation. Not meeting the Hygiene need creates a chance that the animal will fall ill, and causes bad feelings among zoo guests. Not meeting any or all of the remaining three advanced needs—Privacy, Social, and Stimulation—will lower an animal's overall well-being, decreasing its chances for reproducing or behaving happily enough to truly impress zoo guests. However, that's where the consequences stop. Animals that have critical advanced needs stay reasonably happy if all their basic needs are satisfactorily met.

THE PRIVACY NEED

An animal's need for privacy is satisfied when it can spend some time hidden out of sight of the zoo guests. Interestingly, resting in a shelter satisfies the privacy need even though guests can see the animal resting there and have thoughts about how cute it looks sleeping in the shelter.

However, quite a few animals do not use man-made shelters. Appendix A highlights these species; they include such popular animals as the moose and the penguin. When an animal does not use a man-made shelter, there are other ways of providing it with the privacy it requires:

🐾 Building high, solid exhibit fences. Guests can't see through those. Shy animals in high-traffic areas may need high, solid fencing everywhere except in front of the viewing area; others may need just one side of the exhibit closed for viewing. A good way of making sure guests go into viewing areas instead of gawking from zoo paths is to place the viewing area adjacent to the exhibit. Guests will always try to get the best view possible of the animals.

🐾 Modeling habitat terrain so that an animal can hide from view. Even a low rise in the ground that doesn't qualify as a hill can achieve that if you put a dip or a shallow valley on the other side.

🐾 Planting a screen of trees animals can hide behind. This works particularly well if used in conjunction with the low rise mentioned in the previous point.

🐾 Planting certain kinds of plants. Elephant grass can hide a lying-down gazelle or zebra from sight as effectively as anything else; the same applies to cattails for beavers, and larkspur for snow leopards.

> **TIP**
>
> *Provide animals that can swim with deep water in their exhibits. This lets them satisfy both Privacy and Exercise needs.*

All the solutions listed above can be used together in various combinations, as circumstances allow.

SPECIES THAT DON'T USE MAN-MADE SHELTERS

Zoo Tycoon 2 features seven animal species that have no use for man-made shelters. The list above presents recommended moves, but here are some species-specific recommendations:

🐾 **Beaver, crocodile, flamingo:** place a nice body of water in the habitat. Include deep water, with plenty of cattails and gamba grass lining the shore. Use short screens of trees, as well as dips in the ground coupled with cunningly placed rocks and wetland logs. Note that beavers can build themselves shelters if you supply them with sticks (an enrichment object).

🐾 **Moose, okapi:** include hills in the habitat, coupled with a stand or screen of trees. Put a dip in the ground behind a hill and surround it with trees to create an oasis of total privacy (see Figure 4.6).

🐾 **Ostrich:** for the ultimate ostrich haven, raise terrain in a gentle swell with a corresponding dip behind it. Crown the swell with a couple of trees and rocks, and place tall plants in and around the dip.

☝ **Penguin:** this is the hardest species to hide away, especially since you'll almost always have many of these birds. There are no trees in the tundra! Include deep water in the exhibit, and ensure an inlet is hidden behind a rise in the ground or ice; as usual, add a dip behind the rise, and place a few rocks in strategic spots.

Remember also to use solid, high fencing as appropriate! Later on, lining the exhibit fencing with a tall hedge provides privacy for the animals and has a pleasant effect on zoo guests. It becomes an option only with three-star fame, though.

THE HYGIENE NEED

After an animal has fed and drunk, it likes to perform a bit of private business. It will pee or poop (or both) and it will get dirty. If it continues to get dirty until its Hygiene reaches critical status, it may fall ill. If it becomes sick and isn't groomed or washed and healed, it may die. If that happens, it's truly bad news for the watching zoo guests, so you should always be ready to go into action with the brush or the suds and water. Animals that are furry get brushed; others, such as elephants, get washed.

Certain species of animals have particularly high Hygiene needs. All of the bird species are high-maintenance in this respect; half the time spent grooming the animals in your starting, four-exhibit zoo is likely to be spent on peafowl.

Animal hygiene also suffers if the habitat is dirty in general. To make a long, painful story short, your fight for high hygiene consists of diligently raking poop, and grooming and washing animals. You may find yourself doing these tasks more often than you'd like, even if you have a small army of zookeepers. Cleaning up poop is easier if you have a dedicated "restroom" area (see Figure 4.7).

Note that deep water helps satisfy the Hygiene needs of water-loving animals that can swim. For example, keeping a crocodile or a hippo clean becomes much easier if you include enough deep water in its wetlands exhibit. Check Appendix A and the animal entries in the game's Zoopedia for details.

> **TIP**
>
> *Animals prefer to do their after-meal business on a patch of dirt, or rock if dirt is not a feature of their habitat. Provide a suitably private dirt or rock patch within reasonable distance of the food-and-water area.*

FIGURE 4.7:

The family rest-room, panda style.

THE SOCIAL NEED

Animals satisfy their Social needs by interacting with one another. Even animals with high tolerance for solitary life eventually get lonely. The solution is to always adopt a male-and-female pair of any species you acquire. A pair is sometimes less than enough for total satisfaction of Social needs, though. For example, all birds should ideally be adopted in threes, one male and two females; see Chapter 5 for species details.

Acquiring animals in male/female pairs (or greater numbers) carries an instant extra payoff that quickly covers the cost of adopting the second animal. Social interaction between animals is among the stuff zoo guests love to watch the most. Guests get very excited when they see animals calling to each other, playing with each other, and taking care of each other. Animals also interact by grooming each other, which helps meet their Hygiene needs (though it's never enough to take care of them completely).

THE STIMULATION NEED

An animal's Stimulation need can be met in two ways:

- By interacting/playing with other animals

- By playing with animal toys or using enrichment objects

Play-chasing each other counts as top animal entertainment, both for the animals and the guests. Animals also get big-time kicks out of using the more sophisticated enrichment objects.

If an animal's Stimulation need is unmet, it's most likely due to a solitary existence coupled with lack of enrichment object options.

THE SECRET OF EASY NEED SATISFACTION

While reading about animal needs, you must have noticed that in many cases more than one need gets satisfied simultaneously. For example, when two animals are play-chasing, they satisfy Exercise, Social, and Stimulation needs (but increase their Rest need). When one zebra grooms another, the benefits affect both Hygiene and Social needs.

The examples above feature a pair of animals to stress yet again how rewarding it is to adopt more than one animal at a time. If you really want to provide the best possible care for your animals, you will provide them with companions. The rewards of animal interaction benefit everyone: animals are happier, guests are happier, and you'll be happier, too, when you see the increased frequency of visits to your donation boxes.

It's worth noting that some of the most rewarding interactions are those that take place between adult and baby animals. Spectacles such as play-fighting between an adult snow leopard and a snow leopard cub will help satisfy their Exercise, Social, and Stimulation needs while thrilling zoo guests. Given how beneficial happy animal families are to your zoo, there are only two situations in which you'd adopt a single specimen of any species:

- While playing a Campaign scenario, in order to accomplish a given scenario goal (such as "exhibit X species").

👌 Because you're short of funds for a pair, and the solitary animal has to help out with the fundraising work for its own mate. When breeding animals, watch out for territorial conflicts between adult males in the same exhibit! These are most likely to occur when the animals' reproductive urge is close to peaking. Male conflicts do not *have* to occur, but they may, affecting all species from the peaceful gazelles to the big carnivorous cats.

The Rewards of Need Satisfaction

You should *never* allow any of the basic needs to hit critical (red box) status. An animal that has its basic needs largely met enters a blissful state which, given some time, will result in the urge to reproduce. If the reproduction attempt is successful, babies arrive some time later. When they do, numerous new animal behavior options that are multiple-need satisfiers become available. These new animal behaviors will make guests even happier, donation boxes even busier, and so on.

Continue to work on every biome throughout the game until all options for its improvement have been utilized. Unfortunately, this includes continuously helping out your zookeepers in the ongoing battle with poop. You'll find that poop is enemy number one. It makes exhibits dirty and less pleasant for both the animals and the guests; it exerts a constant pressure on the Hygiene need, bringing a chance of sickness. You already know about the mechanics of dealing with poop, monitoring animal need satisfaction, and managing zookeepers from this chapter and from Chapter 2. It's time to leave this stuff behind and look to the future: the new object options and research that let you push animal need satisfaction to higher levels.

NOTE

Before you gain two-star fame, you cannot even plant a single tree in a Tropical Rainforest biome! Since it's a rainforest, total lack of trees makes it somewhat incomplete. However, if you get other factors right, you can still induce the animals within the biome to reproduce.

Improving the Biomes

In *Zoo Tycoon 2*, biome creation isn't an event; it's a process. Prior to the late middle game, it's just not possible to trick out the habitat with the hottest foliage, rocks, animal shelters, and enrichment objects.

You need to press on vigorously to attain two-, then three-star zoo fame as quickly as possible. Both fame levels mark new eras in habitat-object availability. New items include such space-age enrichment objects as the heated rock. Researching the heated rock will set you back $800, purchasing another $1,000, and there will be $50 in monthly upkeep charges thereafter. All such details are noted in Appendix B.

However, here are two important general rules:

🐾 **Trees, plants, and rocks** do not carry research costs. All these habitat-related items become available automatically upon advancing to the required fame level (see Figure 4.8).

🐾 **Animal shelters and enrichment objects** often carry significant research costs and are frequently expensive to purchase, as well. The panda's favorite sleeping place—the hollow tree trunk—will set you back $2,500! That's the price of adopting a pair of camels in the early game. Occasionally, a shelter or toy is available research-free, but you have to pay a stiff purchase price (for example $2,000 for the giraffe house).

FIGURE 4.8:

Shopping for greens becomes exciting upon reaching two-star fame.

Note that it is entirely possible to win five-star fame for your zoo without researching anything. However, researching and obtaining the latest advances that help make animals happier pays for itself quickly. Any money you invest in animal happiness is always invested well!

The next chapter reviews the species in the game, with comments that include more tips on animal care and happiness.

THE ANIMALS WITHIN

HE ANIMALS IN YOUR ZOO ARE A COLLECTION OF UNIQUE CHARACTERS. EACH SPECIES HAS ITS OWN TRAITS THAT MAKE IT UNIQUE. MALE AND FEMALE ANIMALS OF THE SAME SPECIES ARE DIFFERENT, TOO, AND DEMONSTRATE GENDER-ROLE BEHAVIORS: FOR EXAMPLE, ONLY FEMALE TIGERS CARRY TIGER CUBS AROUND IN THEIR MOUTH AND SUCKLE BABY ANIMALS.

THIS CHAPTER REVIEWS EVERY ANIMAL SPECIES IN THE GAME. BASIC STATISTICS ARE FOLLOWED BY A COMMENTARY ON THE ANIMAL'S REQUIREMENTS, TRAITS, AND HABITS, PLUS PRACTICAL TIPS ON ITS IMPORTANCE AND HANDLING IN THE GAME. YOU'LL FIND DETAILED ANIMAL STATS IN APPENDIX A. KEEP IN MIND THAT MANY OF THE ANIMAL COMMENTS IN THIS CHAPTER ARE SUBJECTIVE, AND TREAT THEM AS ADVICE RATHER THAN FINAL VERDICTS DELIVERED FROM A MISTY MOUNTAINTOP. IF YOU PARTICULARLY LIKE A SPECIES, FEEL FREE TO ADOPT IT EVEN IF IT'S JUDGED HERE AS NOT SO HOT. WE ALL HAVE OUR OWN ANIMAL PREFERENCES, SO DON'T LET US DISSUADE YOU FROM YOURS.

ANIMAL PORTRAITS

The species in the game become available at certain fame levels. For your convenience, the species are listed in this chapter in order of their in-game appearance, beginning with half-star fame. This setup lets you see how important fame is in the development of your zoo, and when to plan on expanding a lot (when there are several species worth getting right away) or a little (when there's one species worth getting right away, with others following later).

The number of animal species in your zoo is the single most important factor contributing to your zoo's fame. As a rule, you should acquire as many different species as possible (though some Campaign scenarios disallow adoption, or stress goals unrelated to species diversity). Every new species means greater happiness for your guests, greater fame for your zoo, and more money for yourself. It's a very good deal for everyone concerned.

The animal entries always contain three values: maintenance, guest attraction, and donations. These are *relative* values, so don't let low donations scare you away from adopting an animal. Adopting an animal is almost always worth it, provided you can supply it with proper care. This is where maintenance comes in—as you'll see, different species make different demands on zookeepers. Maintenance values are estimated based on the assumption that exhibits are kept fairly clean; an animal living in a dirty exhibit will need constant grooming.

The guest-attraction factor is derived from the distance a zoo guest is willing to walk to see a given species. Remember that multispecies exhibits are much more attractive than any of the single species they contain. For example, taken separately, most of the savannah species are far from hot with the guests. However, placed together in a big savannah exhibit, they'll generate more money in the donation boxes than a relatively rare species being shown on its own in another exhibit.

Always remember that species sharing a biome type can coexist perfectly in the same exhibit with species from other regions of the world. For example, you can add Australian kangaroos to the African gemsbok's scrub exhibit to create a multispecies Scrub biome (see Figure 5.1). Wetlands animals from Africa happily accept North American vegetation and vice versa, and Bengal tigers feel at home among trees and plants from Africa and South America.

NOTE

Adventurous tycoons may try including predators together with other animals in a suitable biome. You can actually put lions together with gazelles, zebras, and giraffes and see them coexist peacefully—as long as the lions never go hungry!

What matters is that everything is part of the same biome; the region of the world it comes from is unimportant. As a matter of fact, fitting regional vegetation to each animal species is sometimes impossible.

FIGURE 5.1:

Australian and African fauna and flora mix without problems in a scrub exhibit.

FAME:

Every starting zoo in Freeform and Challenge games begins without any animals, and with half-star fame. This fame level gives you adoption rights to four species. Adopting any of the animals in this class costs $1,250, and their availability is almost certain. You can purchase a pair and build a big, suitable exhibit for under $5,000.

The animals that are available at half-star fame aren't strong crowd-pullers. However, this makes them all the more suitable for placing in exhibits close by the zoo entrance, where guests will view them almost automatically.

Note that half-star fame entitles you to three adoption slots on the adoption panel. The four species available at this fame level are the most common species in the game. They're available freely, and you'll see their familiar shapes appear constantly in the adoption slots when playing the adoption lottery.

COMMON PEAFOWL

Biome: Temperate Forest
Maintenance: Very high
Guest Attraction: Very low
Donations: Low

The common peafowl is often one of the first species you adopt in a game. The peafowl will supply you with an educational experience: it will make you understand what the term "high maintenance" means when applied to zoo animals. Like all birds in the game, peafowl produce poop with careless abandon, and need very frequent grooming. They are quite undemanding when it comes to space (50 square tiles for the first bird, and just three more tiles for each extra bird), but tend to multiply rapidly if cared for properly. Given peafowl poop-producing abilities and a relatively small exhibit, you'll find yourself on constant call for emergency cleanups. Limit the number of birds to four to avoid going crazy; two adult males can get along fine with each other.

Although peafowl are cheap to adopt and their temperate forest exhibit isn't expensive, trying to improve these birds' quality of life is costly. Their enrichment objects become available at two-star fame, and they are expensive to research and acquire; the same goes for the peafowl shelter. Outfitting a peafowl exhibit may prove too expensive for quite a while! Try to locate the peafowl next to the moose in the initial stages of the game for maximum neighboring-habitat compatibility.

Statistically, peafowl belong among the least exciting animals on display in your zoo, but guests still get a good kick out of watching them.

TIP

You won't be able to provide peafowl with shelters for quite a while; make sure their habitat includes a screen of trees to give them some privacy.

DROMEDARY CAMEL

Biome: Desert
Maintenance: Very low
Guest Attraction: Very low
Donations: Low

The camel is an excellent choice for beginning tycoons. It is very easy to care for, and its exhibit is cheap and easy to build. It works well next to the savannah exhibit you'll most likely create for another half-star-fame species, the Thomson's gazelle. Although camels are hardly the most exotic animals in the world, guests still like watching them, and you'll see quite a few educational smileys appearing over the audience in front of the camel exhibit (see Figure 5.2). Camels aren't shy, and can seek shelter in the small stable, which is cheap and available at the start of the game.

It's cool to be a camel.

Other endearing camel traits include their very restrained appetites and thirst; they seem to drink even less than they eat. This means low upkeep cost. Given the minimal amount of care they need, camels are quick to procreate; if you start a game with a camel exhibit in place, you may see the first baby camel show up as early as the end of February! However, note that camels require a reasonable amount of space: 70 square tiles for the first camel, 10 more tiles for each extra animal (see Appendix A for the exact space requirements of all the game's animals).

NOTE

Camels are among the longest-lived animals in the game. Your initial pair can outlast two-generation chains of many species.

Camels use the scratching post enrichment object, which is useful in Challenge games: one of the more popular and well-paid early photo challenges requires you to photograph an animal using an enrichment object.

Keep an eye out for a camel spitting on a guest! The victim won't like it, but other guests who see it happen will laugh and point.

MOOSE

Biome: Boreal Forest
Maintenance: High
Guest Attraction: Very low
Donations: Low

This is another animal you'll make fast friends with. Building its exhibit will test your landscaping skills because you'll have to create some sort of natural barrier to provide your moose with privacy. It has no use for man-made shelters—it needs a hill, a screen of trees, or both to satisfy its privacy need. It also appreciates a pond in its habitat, which may be significantly improved once a couple of extra tree types become available at two-star fame. This species has the same space requirements as the camel, and needs a roomy exhibit that lets it run around in spite of the hills and the trees.

The moose exhibit should neighbor the peafowl's for habitat compatibility. It usually makes sense to put the moose and the peafowl to one side of the entrance, and the camel plus the Thomson's gazelle to the other. You'll find yourself quite busy with the moose and peafowl exhibits, especially when compared with the gazelle's and the camel's. While a moose cannot equal a peafowl in the zoo pooping championships, it's still a force to be reckoned with, and a valued contributor to the compost building you'll research and acquire at two-star fame.

The moose uses the scratching post for stimulation, although, just like the camel, it will also happily rub itself against trees. It breeds fairly easily and often.

NOTE

Placing a gift cart next to the moose exhibit results in half the children in the zoo wearing moose hats.

THOMSON'S GAZELLE

Biome: Savannah
Maintenance: Very low
Guest Attraction: Very low
Donations: Low

The Thomson's gazelle is the first of many savannah species you'll adopt in most games. It is a very pleasant-looking and graceful animal (see Figure 5.3), although its guest-attraction factor is among the lowest in the game. It's still a nice addition to a large multispecies savannah exhibit! The exhibit you'll initially build for the gazelles will most likely be remodeled for another species at a later date. This species has a very humble space requirement, needing only as much room as peafowl.

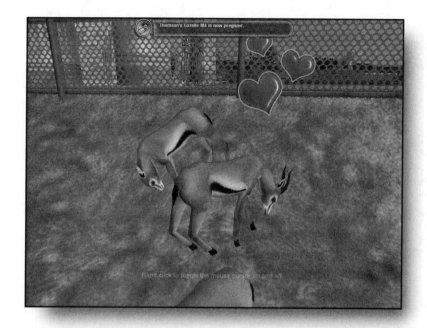

Thomson's gazelles are among the most graceful animals in the game.

Gazelles are easy to care for and often produce a baby gazelle by the third month of a new game. They do not use any enrichment objects, but happily rest in both the small wooden shelter and the small stable that are available at the start of the game. Gazelles can also satisfy their privacy needs by lying down among tall plants; remember that sculpting rises and dips into the terrain helps concealment.

TIP

Gazelles are among the most short-lived animals in the game. Get them breeding fast!

Given the gazelles' graceful and delicate looks, you may be a little shocked to realize that the males of this species can be fiercely territorial. Adult males frequently duel each other when the reproductive urge nears a peak, and it's wise to cull your herd of gazelle regularly by releasing extra males to the wild. Retaining two females and a single male will ensure a high reproduction rate while keeping everybody happy. Remember that guests are distressed to see animals fighting!

FAME: ⭐

It's an extremely pleasant feeling when your young zoo's fame reaches a full star. It opens a fourth adoption slot on the adoption panel, and gives you adoption rights to three new animals. These are all more expensive ($2,000 per specimen) and slightly more difficult to acquire than the half-star-fame set. The new species include two birds that require introducing new types of habitats to

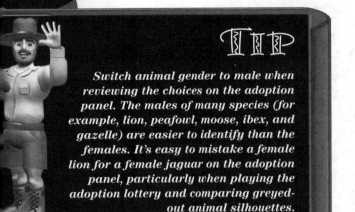

TIP

Switch animal gender to male when reviewing the choices on the adoption panel. The males of many species (for example, lion, peafowl, moose, ibex, and gazelle) are easier to identify than the females. It's easy to mistake a female lion for a female jaguar on the adoption panel, particularly when playing the adoption lottery and comparing greyed-out animal silhouettes.

your zoo; zone the penguin (tundra) in the moose/peafowl wing to minimize habitat conflicts. When building scrub and wetlands exhibits for the gemsbok and flamingo respectively, plan to expand them at a later date to add other species. Most likely, your finances won't let you make them big at this early stage!

Adopting a one-star species is easy given the extra adoption slot, although you'll notice them appearing less frequently than species from the half-star set.

EMPEROR PENGUIN

Biome: Tundra
Maintenance: High
Guest Attraction: Low
Donations: Average

The penguin has many tempting traits: it's the most exotic species of the early adoption choices and has the biggest moneymaking potential. However, it needs quite a lot of attention and doesn't use a man-made shelter. There are no trees in the tundra, so providing enough privacy for your penguins may involve researching the high wooden slat fence.

Penguins are social animals, and they'll feel best if you adopt three—two females and a male. If you adopt a pair, give them plenty of attention, because there are no enrichment objects for penguins at one-and-a-half-star fame. The first enrichment object—a medium ice floe—doesn't become available until two-star fame, and costs a lot to research and acquire. It the most expensive piece of ice you've ever seen (see Figure 5.4).

Penguins require the same amount of space as peafowl, but you'll probably need more room to throw in terrain features such as deep water, which will help your penguins satisfy their Privacy needs. Expanding the exhibit later to include polar bears is an option to keep in mind if you don't have the money to make it big enough right away. Keep in mind that penguins have a healthy appetite, with the usual poop consequences on top of high upkeep costs. A nice feature, however, is that they have long life spans as birds go, outlasting several land species.

Learning how to freeze saltwater carries a price.

GEMSBOK

Biome: Scrub
Maintenance: Low
Guest Attraction: Very low
Donations: Low

The gemsbok is an African species that's virtually trouble-free. It has very moderate eating habits, so it's a good choice if you're still acting as zookeeper to all of your exhibits at this stage of the game. Gemsbok need as much space as camels and moose. If you have plans for your scrub exhibit to include kangaroos later on, allow for a big expansion—kangaroos need a lot of space, too!

Gemsbok like man-made shelters, but don't use any enrichment objects. They have low Stimulation needs, however, and in an adopted pair the animals stay happy just by stimulating each other. Although gemsbok rank very low on the guest-attraction scale, they are a comfortable addition in most games: the other two new species on offer are maintenance-intensive birds.

All in all, this is a somewhat unexciting but reliable species that always looks comfortable in its habitat, producing a steady flow of donation dollars.

GREATER FLAMINGO

Biome: Wetlands
Maintenance: Very high
Guest Attraction: Very low
Donations: Low

The adoption of this graceful bird can be your first step toward building a wetlands exhibit that will eventually grow to contain other species. However, the flamingo has the usual modest bird space requirements, so begin your exhibit modestly, leaving space for expansion later. Remember, you can always remodel the exhibit for a different species. This is important if you're trying to zone the habitats correctly while allowing for biome switches inside certain exhibits.

Flamingoes are entertaining birds that can earn as much donation money as the more exotic penguins. However, they are quite troublesome: they are voracious consumers of expensive shrimp, which, birds being birds, has to be served in dishes (buy two right away). Naturally, this has predictable consequences. Flamingoes are social birds; if you adopt only a pair, be prepared for sulks before babies arrive. These birds need to be groomed frequently (see Figure 5.5); adopting them often marks the point at which you absolutely cannot continue without hiring a zookeeper.

FIGURE 5.5:

Flamingoes seem to get dirty instantly whenever you turn your back.

Flamingoes play with the two types of balls that are available for research at one-star fame, but they are yet another species that does not use man-made shelter. Fortunately, it's possible to trick out a wetlands exhibit with trees, rocks, and plants early in the game.

FAME: ⭐⭐

TIP

Remember to include a fairly decent-sized pond in the flamingo exhibit!

Reaching this zoo fame level wins you adoption rights to three new animal species. These include the very important zebra, which lets you make an addition to your savannah exhibit (or alternatively, build a new, bigger one). The ibex creates an opportunity to build your first alpine exhibit. And you should certainly consider crocodiles if you already have a wetlands exhibit going with flamingoes. However, be warned that, true to their image, crocodiles can be cranky.

Each of the three species that becomes available for adoption at this fame level costs $3,000. Predictably, these three species don't show up in the adoption slots as often as the preceding sets. Getting one may take several "draws," or declines of all species on offer.

COMMON ZEBRA

Biome: Savannah
Maintenance: Low
Guest Attraction: Very low
Donations: Low

Acquiring your zoo's first zebra is always a memorable moment: the little striped horses show well against the savannah background (see Figure 5.6). Adopting a pair of zebras is a financial effort for a one-and-a-half-star-fame zoo, and you'll likely get them one by one. A single zebra can get by for a while with gazelles for company, and the addition of a new species will give your zoo fame a strong boost right away. Also, viewing guests begin dropping extra money in the donation boxes moments after a new species is put on display.

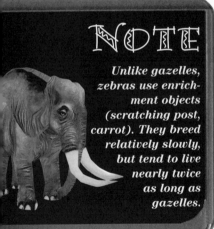

NOTE

*Unlike gazelles,
zebras use enrich-
ment objects
(scratching post,
carrot). They breed
relatively slowly,
but tend to live
nearly twice
as long as
gazelles.*

Zebras tend to blend nicely into your zoo-development plan: they fit the existing savannah exhibit, down to using the small stable for shelter just like the gazelles. They also eat the same food, and their modest space requirements match the gazelles'. The presence of an extra species in an exhibit will markedly increase maintenance of that exhibit; you might have to take the savannah exhibit under personal care until your zoo can afford another zookeeper (it can't at this stage).

Zebras need to be groomed more often than gazelles; fortu-nately, they often groom each other, and each time they do, a few zoo guests reach for their wallets.

IBEX

Biome: Alpine
Maintenance: Average
Guest Attraction: Low
Donations: Average

The ibex presents you with an opportunity to create an Alpine biome, which can work well in the vicinity of the Boreal Forest and Temperate Forest biomes in your zoo (moose and peafowl). This wild mountain goat is a good acquisition: it attracts guests more than any other previously discussed species, and reproduces swiftly when given good care. Creating an easily accessible food-serving area is particularly important because of all the peaks and valleys in this habitat. Otherwise, you'll be besieged by messages about ibex getting stuck on a crag while on their way to a snack.

The ibex needs an amount of attention that's comparable to the moose, partly because it's difficult to chase down all the animals for grooming in the mountains. Cleaning the dreaded poop from the exhibit means plenty of exercise for you; your zookeepers don't do brilliantly in alpine exhibits. Adopting ibex often marks the time you get a second zookeeper; this species earns good donations, and you'll be able to afford new zoo staff (see Figure 5.7).

FIGURE 5.7:
The ibex in your Alpine biome are a pleasant attraction for many zoo guests.

The ibex needs the same amount of space as the moose and the camel; make sure your animals can use all the space in their exhibit by running the Smooth Terrain brush over all surfaces! Ibex use the popular scratching post to enrich their existence, and are happy to rest in the available stables and wooden shelters. Note that you can also improve the Alpine biome right away with trees and plants, although rocks require further advances in fame.

NILE CROCODILE

Biome: Wetlands
Maintenance: High
Guest Attraction: Very low
Donations: Low

The Nile crocodile seems like a nice addition if you've got a wetlands exhibit going. It undoubtedly does its share of transferring money from zoo guests to you, but it is one of the game's most cranky and difficult animals. It's supposed to need the same amount of space as large quadrupeds like the moose and the camel, but it always seems to need slightly more: the crocodile is a rather introverted animal that likes plenty of water, including deep water for both privacy and hygiene. Without enough deep water, keeping crocodiles clean can be a major effort that earns them a high-maintenance label in spite of their relatively restrained pooping activities.

Crocodiles have very long life spans, second only to elephants. The eggs take quite a while to hatch, too! These reptiles carry relatively large upkeep costs, going through beef shanks (enrichment object) at a very quick rate. Researching frozen beef shanks slows down the turnover among croc enrichment objects, but overall this is a slightly troublesome species with a low guest-attraction factor. Check out your exhibit features carefully before deciding to adopt any crocodiles.

FAME:

Two-star fame is when a new era begins in the development of your zoo. Four new species come your way, two of them with relatively strong guest attraction. A new slot opens on the adoption panel, for a total of five. As you know from the previous chapters, two-star fame marks a boost in the number of new guest amenities, as well, including the world-famous family restroom. It's a very busy time for all tycoons, and it will likely be a while before you can afford to adopt one of the newly available species. When you do, there'll be a bit of bad mixed into the good news: all the new animal species except the kangaroo carry a new, higher adoption price tag of $5,500 per animal (the kangaroo stays at $3,000). Naturally, the new species are harder to get than any of the previous ones. They're still available more often than not; a couple of quick runs through the newly expanded adoption slots should yield at least one.

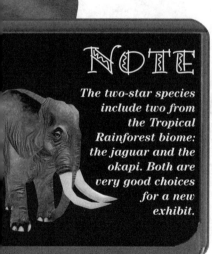

NOTE

The two-star species include two from the Tropical Rainforest biome: the jaguar and the okapi. Both are very good choices for a new exhibit.

The new adoption lineup also includes a third African savannah species: the ostrich. Although expensive, this playful species is a great addition to your big savannah exhibit. The cheaper kangaroo makes a good addition to the gemsbok exhibit. All four new species are winners. You're likely to want the whole set for your zoo in most Freeform and Challenge games.

Jaguar

Biome: Tropical Rainforest
Maintenance: High
Guest Attraction: Low
Donations: Average

The jaguar is your first chance to display one of those bad, baaad carnivorous cats. Actually, you should get a pair: jaguars breed vigorously, and they can help quickly max out the Release into the Wild contribution to zoo fame (see Figure 5.8). Jaguars need slightly more space than any of the animals available earlier.

FIGURE 5.8:

Jaguars are often the first carnivorous cats to appear in your zoo.

Modeling a tropical rainforest habitat for jaguars involves planting plenty of trees. Remember to include a clearing around the food-serving area where the animals can run and play in view of zoo guests. Jaguars prefer the rock cave for shelter, although they'll also gladly rest when hidden from view by trees. You'll have to research the rock cave, and place a pond big enough to swim; jaguars like that form of exercise.

Quite a selection of new enrichment objects becomes available at two-star fame, and several fit the jaguar. Make a point of getting the pink pursuit ball—it's a favorite with many species. Jaguars have healthy appetites, with the usual consequences. Their coats need frequent brushings; four cats will make for a pretty labor-intensive exhibit.

Okapi

Biome: Tropical Rainforest
Maintenance: Low
Guest Attraction: Average
Donations: High

The shy okapi is the first truly exotic species you can display in your zoo. This is reflected by the crowd that quickly gathers to gawk when you unveil your okapi exhibit! It's an animal that commands fat donations—adoption price relative to donation size, it's the best adoption choice in the whole game lineup.

Caring for the okapi calls for a special effort, because this is yet another species that doesn't use a man-made shelter. Fortunately, it's easy enough to create a private oasis of peace in a tropical rainforest habitat. A screen of trees growing on a ridge provides all the privacy needed. Add a hollow behind the ridge if you desire.

TIP

Get your okapi breeding quickly; they aren't exactly short-lived, but they don't live forever, either!

Okapi need quite a lot of space: almost as much as jaguars. They use readily available enrichment objects—fruit in ice, scratching post—and are generally easier to care for than their exotic status would imply. They are a must-have species for all tycoons striving to build a better zoo; given the right environment and enough peace, they breed regularly though quite slowly.

Okapi are happy to have ringtailed lemurs, chimpanzees, and gorillas as companions in the biome. If you manage to assemble a tropical rainforest exhibit displaying all these species together, you'll be bowled over by the number of zoo guests rushing for a look. Place it in the rear half of your zoo to draw guest traffic; it's a combination none will want to miss. Several donation boxes are called for in and around the viewing area.

Ostrich

Biome: Savannah
Maintenance: High
Guest Attraction: Very low
Donations: Low

The playful ostrich is a mandatory addition to your large mixed savannah exhibit. These big birds may not come cheap, but they are worth it. Zoo guests won't be the only ones getting a kick; make a point of strolling around the exhibit in first-person view and listening to ostriches calling to each other!

Unfortunately, ostriches come with the usual bird package: plenty of poop and frequent groomings. A flock of ostriches needs slightly more space than other birds. These birds love to run, and will play-chase each other all over the exhibit. They can also use enrichment objects—the pursuit ball works well here.

Ostriches reproduce regularly once they feel fully at home, and have long life spans as birds go; they live almost as long as rhinos. Adopting ostriches usually marks the point at which you have to dedicate a zookeeper exclusively to the savannah exhibit (see Figure 5.9). You'll have to occasionally jump in with a brush and a rake anyway!

FIGURE 5.9:
Yet another zookeeper for the savannah mega-exhibit.

RED KANGAROO

Biome: Scrub
Maintenance: Low
Guest Attraction: Very low
Donations: Low

This rather charming animal is the big bargain of the two-star lineup: adopting a specimen costs only $3,000. It fits in nicely with the gemsbok in the scrub biome and multiplies quite rapidly. This is good because the kangaroo has one of the shortest life spans in the game; keep an eye on your specimens and release the older ones into the wild regularly. Keep the standard combo of one male and two females to ensure continuing rapid reproduction.

The kangaroo doesn't use a man-made shelter apart from the umbrella shade, but it's an easy-going animal whose privacy needs are easily satisfied.

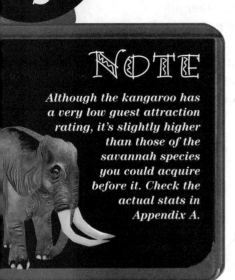

NOTE

Although the kangaroo has a very low guest attraction rating, it's slightly higher than those of the savannah species you could acquire before it. Check the actual stats in Appendix A.

The shared kangaroo/gemsbok exhibit is bound to be large, and fitting in a screen of vegetation without breaking the scrub's barren character isn't a problem. Note that kangaroos find umbrella shades useful, and that the only enrichment object they accept is the short-lived carrot. Replace carrots regularly, checking on the kangaroos' hygiene at the same time. Although they expend quite a bit of effort on grooming and such hygienic activities as dust baths, kangaroos can often use a brushing! Make a point of watching a kangaroo take a dust bath; it's one of the funniest sights in the game.

FAME:

This half-star milestone rewards you with adoption rights to four new species for $7,500 apiece. These are even less readily available than the preceding set, so you'll have to be patient when hunting for them on the adoption panel. All of the choices are good, but three of them are particularly good. This is your chance to acquire giraffes for your savannah exhibit and hippos for the wetlands exhibit. Also, every tycoon will likely be moved to adopt the lion; is a zoo that doesn't display the king of animals truly complete? The cheetah is an attractive species in its own right in spite of outrageous space requirements; however, here it gets a little eclipsed by the other choices.

Note that if you're a daring tycoon, you might try putting the lions and the cheetahs together with the herbivores in your huge savannah exhibit (it has to be huge—think double the necessary space allotment for every animal!). If you do, it's strongly recommended you build several carnivore restaurants in the exhibit, and monitor the situation closely. If you take very good care of the carnivores and everyone has plenty of space, peace will reign in the exhibit and enthusiasm will rule outside it. Put in a couple of extra donation boxes!

CHEETAH

Biome: Savannah
Maintenance: Average
Guest Attraction: Low
Donations: Average

The swift cheetah needs more space than any other species in the game, and you'll see why when you watch it run! Unfortunately, this is the primary argument against adopting it, particularly if you're building a zoo on a smaller map. Placing the cheetah exhibit along one of the zoo's side walls is probably the most feasible solution. When setting up the savannah habitat, leave a path for the fast runners; a classic stadiumlike ellipse circling the exhibit works nicely.

Cheetahs have the ability to pull in fat donations, especially when they're running around. They also enjoy using a range of enrichment objects, as shown in the Zookeeper's Recommendations; once again, the pursuit ball gives great value for the money.

One unhappy fact about the cheetahs is that they have short life spans. However, if you make them happy in your zoo, you'll find that they multiply very quickly: there will be no shortage of champion runners!

NOTE

Watching cheetahs fooling around with a ball or chasing each other is one of the game's most entertaining sights.

HIPPOPOTAMUS

Biome: Wetlands
Maintenance: Very high
Guest Attraction: Low
Donations: Average

The hippopotamus is a good reason to either expand or build a wetlands exhibit. Once you adopt a couple of these animals, make sure you stand beside them in first-person view and listen to them yawn (see Figure 5.10). Entertainment aside, the hippo isn't an easy animal to care for: it's a voracious

FIGURE 5.10:

It's a pity you never heard of mouthwash.

93

eater and pooper with a high Hygiene need. However, it has a long life span and reproduces quite easily; baby hippos take a long time to reach adulthood, thus giving the exhibit a baby attractiveness bonus for a long while.

Hippos require adequate space—their requirements are actually modest for animals of such size, equaling those of gorillas or ibex. They do, however, require a large body of water (including deep water), where they like to exercise. This also helps greatly in satisfying their Hygiene need. Hippos rest well in a large concrete shelter, which needs to be researched before it can be acquired.

Note that all the bother you may have with hippo poop has a silver lining if you own a compost building. The profits these big animals generate via the compost building go a long way toward paying for their food.

LION

Biome: Savannah
Maintenance: High
Guest Attraction: Low
Donations: Average

The lion is yet another savannah species from Africa. It's a big eater, pooper, and breeder, in addition to being the legendary king of animals. It really deserves its own exhibit and enough care to begin producing lion cubs. The lion's life span leaves much to be desired—you'd better set about breeding quickly.

There's always plenty of action in a biome populated by lions and their children, so the donation volume tends to be high. Like cheetahs, lions can use a very wide range of enrichment objects. Keeping these animals' Stimulation need satisfied isn't a problem if you have the cash required to research and purchase nice lion toys like the post and rope with ice, or a heated rock.

You'll likely adopt a pair of lions as much for your own enjoyment as for your guests'. Dropping in on the lion exhibit and listening to the majestic beasts roar is an interesting experience! You'll have it many times while dealing with the royal poop.

RETICULATED GIRAFFE

Biome: Savannah
Maintenance: Low
Guest Attraction: Low
Donations: Average

The giraffe is a surprisingly low-maintenance animal for its size. It adds plenty of life to your big multispecies savannah exhibit, exerting a major influence on donations (see Figure 5.11). In large part, this is thanks to this animal's

long neck, which makes even everyday actions such as eating and drinking entertaining for the eager zoo guests. You'll be truly entertained, too, when you watch a giraffe running around with ostriches, zebras, and gazelles. A well-maintained savannah exhibit containing these species and complete with baby animals can make guests donate close to their entire wad in one magnificent gesture.

FIGURE 5.11:
Ah, those graceful necks.... Zoo guests love to watch giraffes in action, whatever the action might be.

Giraffes require an astonishingly modest amount of space (not much more than peafowl). However, the giraffe house shelter takes up plenty, plus it's expensive to research and acquire. You'll need it, though—it's hard to guarantee giraffes the necessary amount of privacy otherwise.

FAME:

Three-star fame marks another great milestone in the development of your zoo. You receive adoption rights to four new species, which include yet another African savannah animal with a relatively high attraction factor: the black rhino. There's a big jump in the number of adoption slots available—from five to seven! You'll really need those extra slots, too, because the animals from the three-star set aren't easy to come by. Your chance of seeing one of the new species turn up in an adoption slot is smaller than the chances for the previous animals.

Each animal made available at three-star fame carries the same stiff price: $10,000.

AMERICAN BEAVER

Biome: Wetlands
Maintenance: Average
Guest Attraction: Average
Donations: High

The beaver has astonishing donation-pulling power for such a little feller. You can put it into a very spacious wetlands exhibit to coexist happily with hippos and crocodiles, but somehow that doesn't look right. The beaver is a sociable animal, and feels happiest when there are at least two other beavers sharing the exhibit. However, you can adopt a pair and work the usual magic with loving care, inducing the beavers to reproduce and find new happiness in numbers.

Remember to put plenty of water, including deep water, in the beavers' wetlands exhibit!

Beavers do not use man-made shelters, and you must take care to ensure them enough privacy; they need a fair amount. Luckily, even plants such as cattails are helpful in hiding this small critter from the public eye, and fitting out the beaver exhibit with a well-placed screen of trees provides enough seclusion. On the other hand, beavers require as much space as many considerably larger animals. Given their rapid reproduction under the right conditions, you may quickly be faced with exhibit overcrowding. This always comes as a bit of a shock, because the beaver exhibit appears to be half empty most of the time. Monitor beaver numbers through the Quick Stats panel! In spite of a relatively short life span, beavers have a sneaky tendency to accumulate unseen because of their brisk reproduction rate, most often with two baby animals per litter.

Beavers enjoy the use of a unique enrichment object called sticks, affordably priced at $200. Given sticks, beavers perform a little bit of magic and build their own shelters: beaver lodges. This greatly entertains zoo guests.

BLACK RHINOCEROS

Biome: Savannah
Maintenance: Very high
Guest Attraction: Below average
Donations: Average

The black rhino is an imposing African savannah species that will drive home the point, yet again, that it's wise to build very big savannah exhibits (see Figure 5.12). The rhino needs lots of space—almost as much as a cheetah. It provides the big savannah exhibit with plenty of extra guest pull and is very successful at persuading guests to empty their wallets into the nearest donation box after they've been watching for a while. Once you place rhinos in the savannah exhibit, install an ATM nearby! Some guests will need to withdraw more money to afford gifts from the cart after getting carried away by the enthusiasm to donate.

Take it easy, guy—I just want to wash you.

The rhino reproduces slowly but has one of the longest life spans in *Zoo Tycoon 2*. It also proudly ranks as one of the top three contributors to the profitability of your compost building. If you don't want to be swooping down on the Savannah biome every few minutes, hire an extra *dedicated* zookeeper to take care of things. He'll be plenty busy, and you'll be adding elephants to the savannah soon, anyway.

Rhinos are one of two species that have the ability to knock down fencing if they're angry (the other is elephants). However, this won't ever happen in your expertly run zoo, so placing rhinos in exhibits with low chain-link fencing won't be a problem.

POLAR BEAR

Biome: Tundra
Maintenance: High
Guest Attraction: Average
Donations: High

Polar bears can share the penguin exhibit—if it's big enough. Both species need plenty of space; the polar bear's space requirement falls just short of the cheetah's. Since both species are quite attractive to zoo guests, putting penguins and polar bears in separate but adjoining exhibits may be the best solution. It lets you merge the exhibits into one and split them up again with great ease. It's tundra all around, and there is no habitat clash.

Polar bears are big eaters and compost producers, and they need plenty of exercise. You must remember to include an expanse of water in their habitat; this is a species that likes deep water! Polar bears enjoy using a wide range of enrichment objects: balls, frozen food, an artistically shaped ice floe, and a blue plastic barrel are all appreciated. If your grand plan includes adopting some single specimens of a few species, the polar bear is a good candidate: it doesn't mind living alone and has a reasonably long life span.

NOTE

The polar bear breeds well and surprisingly briskly, but you must remember to build a truly big exhibit.

You can bring a little extra joy into a polar bear's life by feeding it food off a fancy plate such as the rack of ribs, a.k.a. artificial animal carcass, stuffed with fish or meat. Juicy! Outfit the polar bear exhibit with a snowy cave (prior research needed) for extra animal comfort.

RINGTAILED LEMUR

Biome: Tropical Rainforest
Maintenance: Low
Guest Attraction: Low
Donations: Average

The ringtailed lemur is a very useful little cutie that can be placed in an okapi exhibit instantly, thus creating a multispecies Tropical Rainforest biome that will wow zoo guests big-time. It has modest space requirements and is very playful. It can make good use of a range of enrichment objects, thus making up for the okapi's unremarkable guest-entertainment value. You, too, will find it pretty amusing to see a lemur chasing a pursuit ball bigger than itself! It's interesting to note that the ringtailed lemur shares a passion for lookout posts with the peafowl, and is fond of figs, like chimps and gorillas.

Lemurs have an acceptable life span and reproduce easily if receiving proper care. These bouncy little critters can sometimes have their Hygiene needs unmet because they are forever climbing trees and hiding in the branches, making it difficult for zookeepers to reach them. They are easy to keep happy, though, thanks to the nice selection of tasty dishes you'll be able to provide for them. Lemur favorites include substrate piles, elevated food dishes, and such culinary tours de force as hollow logs stuffed with apples—all served at no charge. It's good to be a lemur (see Figure 5.13)!

It's good to be a lemur, a lemur with fresh figs.

FAME:

This zoo-fame level marks the introduction of three new and relatively rare species. Two of these—the Bengal tiger and the grizzly bear—may be adopted as single specimens without subsequent big trouble with Social needs. The chimpanzee adds even more power to your multispecies Tropical Rainforest biome. Adopting any of the animals in this small group costs $15,000, and you need some luck to draw their ticket when playing the adoption lottery.

BENGAL TIGER

Biome: Tropical Rainforest
Maintenance: High
Guest Attraction: Below average
Donations: Average

The Bengal tiger is a very good choice for a small, single-specimen exhibit. Naturally, breeding Bengal tigers can be even more rewarding, but tycoons sometimes have to make hard choices, particularly when playing Campaign scenarios with tough goals.

TIP

Tigers like to have plenty of space, plenty of trees, and enough water for a refreshing swim.

Tigers have disappointingly short life spans, so keeping a single specimen around for a long time may prove expensive! If you choose to breed them, two cubs are usually born following a short pregnancy. The maturing period is fairly long, giving the tiger exhibit a little extra zip and zowie with the paying public. Tigers are playful creatures and enjoy using a range of enrichment objects; that old standby, the pursuit ball, is as popular as with other species. Adult and juvenile male tigers enjoy play-fighting, but adults sometimes get down to real violence when reproductive urges peak for two males sharing an exhibit. When a juvenile male turns into an adult, it may be time to release the older male into the wild.

CHIMPANZEE

> **Biome:** Tropical Rainforest
> **Maintenance:** Very high
> **Guest Attraction:** Above average
> **Donations:** High

The chimpanzee is a very desirable though troublesome species. It has a relatively high guest-attraction factor that's strong enough to inspire guest pilgrimages to a dedicated chimp exhibit. When you put chimps together with lemurs and okapis, your multispecies tropical rainforest biome can instantly become the hottest thing in your zoo. To fully exploit the coming miniwindfall, place a couple of extra donation boxes and a gift shop in the vicinity of the tropical rainforest exhibit's viewing area.

The spectacular rewards of adopting chimpanzees come with a downside. Chimps demand quality care. They have high Social and Stimulation needs—don't even think about adopting a single chimp! They need grooming very frequently, and if they don't get it, they quickly fall ill. Breeding chimps requires getting a dedicated zookeeper for the mixed tropical rainforest exhibit, and even then, your timely assistance will be required once in a while.

Chimps have modest space requirements (same as the peafowl's), and a very long life span if they're kept healthy. A short pregnancy is followed by a lengthy juvenile period, so the chimps' pulling power is further enhanced by the long-term presence of baby and juvenile animals. Chimps are very much into animal toys of all kinds, and are fond of culinary delicacies such as figs (enrichment object) and hollow logs stuffed with apples, bananas, honey, or yummy insects (see Figure 5.14). Substrate piles and elevated food dishes, comfy sleeping

baskets, fancy toys such as painting easels, and monkey bars that cost a pile just to research are some of the props useful for keeping chimps happy in your zoo.

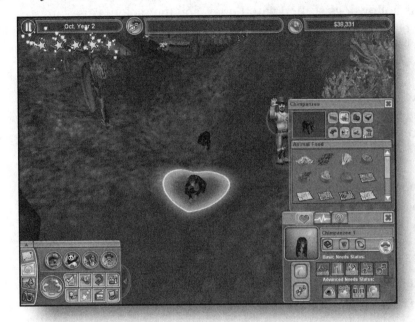

GRIZZLY BEAR

Biome: Boreal Forest
Maintenance: High
Guest Attraction: Average
Donations: High

The grizzly bear is another species that can be exhibited solo without lonely-heart blues. As usual, breeding grizzly bears brings greater rewards, but a Campaign scenario or a short-term strategic goal may make adopting a single grizzly a good solution.

NOTE

Gift carts with their stuffed bears usually do very well next to grizzly exhibits.

Grizzly bears inhabit an environment identical to that of another North American species, the moose. They like plenty of mixed trees, plants, rocks, hills, and a pond big enough for a swim. Grizzlies live to a ripe old age; when breeding, a pregnancy of average length is followed by a long juvenile period. Naturally, this means prolonged presence of baby animals for your zoo guests. Note that grizzlies cause guests to be very generous when giving donations to the zoo. It's not a trouble-free species to acquire and maintain, but it's worth it.

Grizzly bears need plenty of space—even more than moose. They are fond of a range of enrichment objects, including balls, frozen food, and exotic luxuries such as the heated rock. They can be made happier by eating a range of delicacies such as hollow logs stuffed with honey, and the rack of ribs—an artificial carcass container with meat.

FAME: ★★★★

When your zoo achieves four-star fame, it has reached the last milestone on the way to five-star glory. Four-star status is rewarded with four very rare species and two more slots on the adoption panel, for a total of nine. You'll truly appreciate the extra slots, because hunting for one of the four-star animals can be a long process.

Adopting a four-star animal always costs $20,000. However, this expense is fully justified in longer games, in which these expensive acquisitions have the time to pay back the investment with increased guest donations.

AFRICAN ELEPHANT

Biome: Savannah
Maintenance: Very high
Guest Attraction: Above average
Donations: High

The African elephant is the crowning glory of your multispecies savannah exhibit. Unfortunately, it's pretty high-maintenance; adding it to numerous other animals often necessitates adding a third zookeeper dedicated to the savannah exhibit. The elephant also needs to be washed frequently, and if you get two in an attempt to breed, you'll have to lend a hand, even with three zookeepers in the exhibit. This will be partly because your zookeepers will be constantly interrupting their cleaning and grooming activities to replenish food supplies. The elephant-led assembly of creatures in the savannah exhibit will be going through food at record pace!

Elephants can be treated with several delicacies and fancy tableware — substrate piles, elevated dishes, and browse holders. Enrichment objects include the painting easel and the interesting-looking peanut holder, whose research alone costs a cool $1,000 (see Figure 5.15). That's also how much you'll have to pay for researching the elephant house, which is this species' favored shelter. An elephant house takes up a lot of space; it's big, as is everything that's associated with elephants. Naturally, it also takes a big budget to adopt, satisfy, and breed these animals.

FIGURE 5.15:

It takes plenty of money to conceive the perfect peanut dispenser.

Caring for elephants may mean extra trouble, but all your little sacrifices won't be in vain. Zoo guests never fail to be impressed by clean, healthy, happy elephants creating masterpieces worthy of van Gogh. The local ATM and donation boxes receive a workout; let this be your consolation as you approach another pile with your trusty rake.

Elephants appreciate a pool of water big enough for them to engage in spraying water over themselves.

Mountain Gorilla

Biome: Tropical Rainforest
Maintenance: Very high
Guest Attraction: Above average
Donations: High

The elephant tops off your multispecies savannah exhibit with a magnificent flourish; the mountain gorilla does the same for your multispecies tropical rainforest exhibit. Seeing okapi, lemurs, chimps, and gorillas all in the same exhibit drives zoo guests bananas—get ready for messages announcing your zoo is short of ATMs. The gorilla is a finicky animal that requires plenty of attention and expense to stay happy, but the game is fair and the rewards are more than worth it.

Gorillas have a healthy space requirement, equal to a moose's. Given good care, they reproduce regularly: an average-length pregnancy is followed by a long juvenile period during which watching guests are treated to many

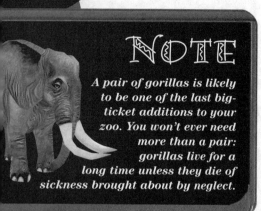

A pair of gorillas is likely to be one of the last big-ticket additions to your zoo. You won't ever need more than a pair: gorillas live for a long time unless they die of sickness brought about by neglect.

entertaining displays. Predictably, gorillas can be fed a wide range of tasty foods on fancy tableware, just like chimps; delicacies such as figs and carrots act as enrichment objects along with painting easels. Remember to set these up within sight of the guest viewing area!

RED PANDA

Biome: Temperate Forest
Maintenance: Very high
Guest Attraction: High
Donations: Very high

The red panda is one of the three very rare Asian animals that top the adoption list in *Zoo Tycoon 2*. Acquiring this species and taking care of it is a good dress rehearsal for handling the giant panda, which follows soon: acquisition of the rare red pandas is often the decisive step that pushes your zoo into five-star fame. Red pandas share habitat tastes with giant pandas, and the two species can be kept together in a very large Temperate Forest biome tricked out with the best in vegetation, rocks, and animal enrichment objects. Red pandas have a variety of expensive tastes, starting with fancy dishes of bamboo (served on substrate piles), and ending with their preferred shelter: the hollow tree stump, at merely $2,500 a pop. To put it in perspective, a pair of half-star-fame animals costs the same amount.

Red pandas are an irresistible draw for zoo guests; they are perfectly capable of drawing guests into the deepest reaches of your zoo without assistance from other nearby species. Unfortunately, their life span is very short, and their high adoption price makes breeding the only sensible option. A short pregnancy most often results in a litter of two cubs, which grow up after a relatively short juvenile period (see Figure 5.16).

Ostrich 17 has just hatched.

Right click to toggle the mouse cursor on and off.

FIGURE 5.16:

Baby red pandas are cute little devils.

Pandas are playful animals if kept happy through attentive care. The enrichment objects they enjoy are a small cross section of the objects found in the game: they include standbys such as the scratching post, balls, and the rubber toy, and the high-tech heated rock.

SNOW LEOPARD

Biome: Alpine
Maintenance: High
Guest Attraction: High
Donations: Very high

TIP

When taking care of very rare and sensitive animals like the scarce Asian species, keeping the exhibit clean and the animals groomed assumes even more importance than usual. Check on their exhibits once in a while even if they have a dedicated zookeeper!

The snow leopard is the most exotic predator available in the game. It's one of the two animals from the Alpine biome, and simply replacing the ibex with this species may be a good move if you're playing a smaller map, where space is at a premium. The snow leopard needs lots of space—just slightly less than the cheetah. While keeping a single specimen happy is possible, the short life span of this animal may force you to spend $20,000 on a replacement in a longer game.

Any competent tycoon can breed snow leopards. The only possible serious obstacle is lack of space in the exhibit. A short pregnancy is most often followed by the birth of two cubs. The juvenile period is relatively short, but during that time, the already considerable donations outside the snow leopard exhibit will grow faster than the cubs. The snow leopard engages in a full range of interactions with its offspring, and as you already know, activities such as play-fighting are highly entertaining to zoo guests.

The snow leopard enjoys playing with a range of animal enrichment objects that includes the old stalwart scratching post, as well as high-tech gimmicks such as the post and rope with block of ice, or the heated rock. The food choices available are refreshingly modest: no elevated dishes here, although there is the appetizing animal carcass stuffed with meat or fish.

FAME: ★★★★★

Finally, after months of effort, your zoo has reached five-star fame! You gain adoption rights to just one new species: the infamous giant panda. Adoption price: a mere $50,000 per animal. The number of open adoption slots stays at nine. Managing to adopt a giant panda may mean many, many empty draws in the adoption lottery!

GIANT PANDA

Biome: Temperate Forest
Maintenance: Very high
Guest Attraction: Extremely high
Donations: Very high

This is it, the Holy Grail of tycoons worldwide: a giant panda in your zoo. No, make that two pandas—which, given your skill, shall shortly result in a third.

When the big hour strikes and you finally get to place a giant panda or two in your luxury temperate forest exhibit, you'll find that this is indeed the most picky and sensitive of all species in the game. The giant panda exhibit should have a dedicated zookeeper if there's to be any breeding going on. You, too, will have to step in repeatedly to groom the animals.

Giant pandas fit well in a hilly temperate forest habitat wooded with trees and bamboo and featuring a peaceful, moist hollow with water. Pandas are very shy and it's a good idea to model the habitat features so as to give the animals maximum privacy (see Figure 5.17). At the same time, the hollow tree stump that the pandas use as shelter should be visible from the guest viewing area so that onlookers will feel inspired to give you even more money. Put the tree-stump shelters and the food-serving area in plain view of the zoo guests, but plant enough trees elsewhere to let the panda lurk unseen whenever the mood takes it.

A giant panda wandering among the foliage of its deluxe habitat.

Giant pandas have an average life span that is easily threatened by illnesses. Buying giant panda replacements is affordable for a five-star zoo, but of course you'll do your best to breed the giant panda yourself. It won't be hard if you simply take care of the animals' every need, and wait patiently. An average pregnancy is followed by the birth of a single cub, which takes quite a while to reach adulthood. No other animal has anywhere near the guest-attraction factor of baby giant pandas. Checking the actual attraction data in Appendix A will give you an idea of how attractive giant panda cubs appear when compared with other species: They're 50% better than adult giant pandas, which are already irresistible.

Giant pandas have a very modest taste in food, eating bamboo shoots exclusively. They are similarly restrained with enrichment objects, using none of the high-tech gadgets that exotic predators favor. Balls, the rubber toy, the tire, the plastic barrel, and the scratching post—these are the giant panda's rustic preferences.

NOTE

Breeding giant pandas is the goal of the Campaign game's final stand-alone scenario.

FREEFORM AND CHALLENGE GAMES

ZOO TYCOON 2 LETS YOU PLAY FREEFORM OR CHALLENGE GAMES ON A WIDE VARIETY OF MAPS. THE MAP SET FOR EITHER TYPE OF GAME INCLUDES ALL 10 BIOMES FEATURED IN ZOO TYCOON 2. SELECTING A BIOME TYPE IN THE FREEFORM OR CHALLENGE GAME MENU LETS YOU CHOOSE FROM MAPS FEATURING THAT BIOME TYPE. THERE ARE AT LEAST THREE (SMALL, MEDIUM, LARGE), AND OFTEN FOUR (THE THREE MAP SIZES PLUS ONE EXTRA MAP WITH A SPECIAL FEATURE—FOR EXAMPLE, A COASTLINE). THE GRASSLAND BIOME TYPE, HOWEVER, HAS NO FEWER THAN SEVEN MAPS! IN ADDITION, THE BIOME SQUARES MAP, SO USEFUL FOR LEARNING THE GAME, IS WITHIN THE GRASSLAND MAP SET.

THIS CHAPTER REVIEWS FREEFORM AND CHALLENGE GAMES. PLAYING A CHALLENGE GAME IS MUCH MORE DIFFICULT: UNLIKE FREEFORM GAMES, CASH IS LIMITED—THOUGH YOU CAN SET THE LIMIT ANYWHERE FROM $5,000 TO SEVERAL MILLION DOLLARS. ANIMALS, STRUCTURES, AND OBJECTS BECOME AVAILABLE ONLY ONCE YOUR ZOO HAS REACHED A CERTAIN LEVEL OF FAME; ACQUIRING MANY STRUCTURES INVOLVES PRIOR RESEARCH, TOO. THEREFORE, MOST OF THIS CHAPTER FOCUSES ON CHALLENGE GAMES, AND INCLUDES A WALKTHROUGH THAT HELPS YOU GET YOUR ZOO OFF THE GROUND WHEN STARTING WITH ONLY $5,000. NOTE THAT TYPES OF CHALLENGES ARE LISTED, WITH APPROPRIATE COMMENTS, IN APPENDIX C.

FREEFORM GAMES

Freeform games offer you the freedom to do whatever you want to in two ways. You get unlimited cash, and you have access to all of the game's animals, structures, and objects (though special unlockable objects won't appear until you've earned them) without having to lift a finger. These two features mean that Freeform games are the ideal choice for you when your goal is to do one of the following:

- **Learn about the game.** You have instant access to all the game's features. Unlimited cash means mistakes don't cost anything but time. This means Freeform isn't the best choice when you want to learn how to play the game *well*. When mistakes don't hurt, they're harder to remember and easier to repeat.

- **Learn zoo layout and design.** The Freeform mode allows you to experiment as much as you want to with zoo design. Design experiments are expensive and risky; a Freeform game is your chance to see whether you can come up with a zoo layout that beats anything suggested in Chapter 2 of this book or on *ZT2* websites. Good zoo layout means placing big guest attractions in strategic spots to improve zoo traffic; the unlimited cash lets you move structures around as much as you want.

- **Design a perfect zoo.** You may want to participate in one of the contests organized by the *Zoo Tycoon* community; for example, to build the best-looking zoo you can, or to hit a record number of zoo guests. Or you might simply want to build a special zoo for your own enjoyment, a little masterpiece of beauty and functionality that makes you think, "Hmmm. Looks like I'm the greatest, after all." (Freeform is also very good for creating funny or interesting situations to photograph—animals stalking and hunting, guests getting attacked, etc.)

- **Create a zoo for the first-person (guest) view.** If you want to build the perfect zoo for taking a stroll and photographing various spectacular views and events, Freeform is the way to go. Winding paths, waterfalls, hills, and valleys are mostly a hindrance during goal-oriented play in a Campaign scenario or a Challenge game. Time and time again, you'll have to sacrifice first-person-view beauty for practical reasons. Freeform games allow you to spend as much as you like on zoo decor, and hire enough zookeepers and maintenance workers to keep you from being bothered by emergency messages during your visit to your own zoo.

Freeform games are also perfect for nailing solutions to problems encountered in Campaign and Challenge games. You can find out how a plan of yours works out in practice before you apply it in another scenario. You can rehearse certain moves, such as building a big multispecies exhibit, to nail down its cost and optimum size (see Figure 6.1). And you have the freedom to conduct various interesting experiments, such as seeing how long it takes for a lion to start chasing guests after you've taken away its food and removed part of its exhibit barrier.

FIGURE 6.1:
Practice building complex exhibits in the Freeform mode.

CHOOSING A FREEFORM MAP

You should select the map that fits the game goal you've set for yourself. If you're learning exhibit design, choose a small map, and the biome type that fits the animals you have in mind. If you're working on zoo layouts, choose a medium or large map with hills and valleys; that will force you to use terrain-modifying tools and encourage you to build raised pathways and sunken exhibits. Modifying zoo terrain may be free of charge, but as explained in Chapter 2, it's an art that requires a lot of practice.

If your system is powerful enough to handle huge zoos, large-map Freeform games offer the perfect opportunity to really spread your wings as a zoo designer and builder. You should play at least a couple of games on large

Freeform maps before you go for a five-star-fame zoo in a Challenge game. As explained in Chapter 2, good zoo-design solutions for large maps are different from medium- and small-map zoo layouts.

Here are three rough rules for choosing map size:

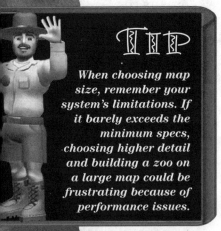

TIP

When choosing map size, remember your system's limitations. If it barely exceeds the minimum specs, choosing higher detail and building a zoo on a large map could be frustrating because of performance issues.

TIP

You can choose the map you want to play by clicking directly on its location on the globe in the center of the Freeform game screen. Rotate the globe with the hand cursor that appears when you hold down the left mouse button.

- **Small maps** are good for learning the basics. Play a small map if you want to get used to the interface and to moving around in first-person view. Small maps also let you learn where to place basic zoo structures (donation boxes especially), and how to satisfy the needs of everyone in your zoo. Furthermore, they are perfect for improving your exhibit-design skills.

- **Medium maps** are especially good for almost everything else to do with learning and experimenting. They are perfect for improving your zoo-layout skills, although, as mentioned earlier, medium-map layouts aren't optimum choices for large maps. They are also a very good choice for players who want to build a larger zoo while running the game on a relatively slow system.

- **Large maps** are the right choice when you aim for perfection on a lavish scale. If you ever attempt to build the world's best zoo, build it on a large Freeform map.

CHALLENGE GAMES

Challenge games make use of the same maps as Freeform games, but they play very differently. As you would expect, they feature numerous tests of your tycoon skills. Here are the challenging features:

- **Limited cash.** You may set your starting cash to any round sum between $5,000 and several million dollars. The default is $30,000, which enables you to get your zoo off to a roaring start, with four exhibits and all the available guest amenities and decor. Since you bought this guide, you're an ambitious tycoon who appreciates a challenge, and you'll most likely be starting with $5,000. You'll find advice for a $5,000 Challenge game later in this chapter.

If you start a Challenge game with $5,000, you'll need to recycle some zoo objects to complete initial construction work. Building an exhibit of decent size, a stretch of path, plus an animal-viewing area, and setting up a donation box will likely leave you short of money for your first pair of animals. Recycling is discussed later in the chapter.

- **Photo-safari challenges.** Photo-safari challenges require you to take two or more photographs (usually two to four) of specific zoo features and/or zoo events. They are almost always great opportunities to boost your finances or zoo fame. You'll find a full list of the game's photo challenges in Appendix C; in the meantime, be warned that taking on certain challenges can be a bad move, and that timing is a factor. Accepting the wrong challenge at the wrong time may mean it will take a very long time to complete.

- **Limited animal-adoption/zoo structure options.** You'll have to earn your right to more options by increasing your zoo fame. Greater zoo fame means access to exotic animal species, more adoption choices on the adoption panel, and a wider selection of zoo structures and objects. Taking advantage of these new options helps increase you zoo's fame. Note that you must still research many of the new zoo structures and objects (for example, new types of fencing or guest amenities) before you can build them. Your newly improved fame simply makes them available for research. Other fame-related zoo objects, such as new trees, don't need to be researched. Appendices A and B list what becomes available when, and any costs involved.

Challenge games are the perfect choice to really hone your tycoon skills. Needless to say, you'll become a first-class zoo-fame hound, eagerly sniffing for opportunities to increase animal and guest happiness. You do remember that in *ZT2* more happiness all around means more money for you, don't you? If not, take a look at Figure 6.2.

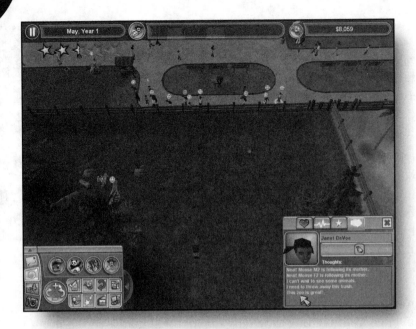

A little sea of twenty-dollar smiles.

SETTING STARTING MONEY

Challenge games play very differently depending on the amount of starting money you've awarded yourself. The default amount of $30,000 makes for a game of moderate difficulty. You can instantly build everything there is to build at half-star fame, and continue to develop your zoo at a rapid pace. Giving yourself even more money at the start will result in faster zoo development. When you set the amount to over $100,000, your Challenge game will play almost like a Freeform game with challenges attached. You might have to wait a bit before acquiring the more expensive animals, that's all.

Setting starting money in Challenge games is also determined by the size of the chosen map. As a rule, the smaller the map, the more money you should award yourself. You'll be playing small maps principally to learn the Challenge part of the game, so feel free to allocate yourself a fat wad. You'll be playing medium maps to hone your skills, so award yourself a medium-fat wad. When you get to large maps, be brave and start with minimum money (especially since you get all that extra cash from recycling).

Here's what to expect at certain starting-money settings:

- **$30,000:** This is a good setting for newcomers to the *Zoo Tycoon* series and/or relatively new gamers. Basically, it lets you fritter away half your starting money and still get your zoo off to a healthy start. If you waste

less, you'll be able to kick off your zoo with all four animal species available at the start of the game, plus an array of guest conveniences and amenities. You'll be able to hire a zookeeper and maintenance worker right away. If you don't waste money, expect your zoo to hit two-star fame within a month or two of opening.

$20,000: This is a good choice for more-experienced gamers who are new to the *Zoo Tycoon* series. It lets you get your zoo off to a good start; if you don't waste money, you'll still be able to adopt all four available animal species right away. You can afford enough zoo-guest conveniences and amenities to hit three-star fame within a month or two. You might not be able to afford a zookeeper right away—this means performing zookeeper tasks yourself in first-person view. You *can* afford a maintenance worker, and you should hire one if you are looking after two or more exhibits.

$5,000: This is a good choice for gamers familiar with the *Zoo Tycoon* series. You'll face an exciting test of your tycoon skills! You cannot waste any money when building your exhibit. Yes, you'll be able to afford just a single exhibit to begin with, but given your superior tycoon skills, that's no problem. A large map should yield enough recycling cash to buy at least some guest conveniences and amenities right away—but don't forget to put in *one* donation box in a strategic spot before anything else! You won't be able to hire a zookeeper or a maintenance worker right away; a maintenance worker usually becomes affordable after a month, a zookeeper after two months. This is perfectly okay if you have no more than three exhibits to look after.

In game terms, each extra $5,000 in starting money translates to roughly one month in zoo development time (assuming you don't waste any money on the way). A starting zoo created with $30,000 is comparable to a how a zoo created with $5,000 will be six months down the road (see Figure 6.3). That's assuming you won't make/lose money through taking on challenges. Yes, you can lose money on those if you aren't careful; such possible pitfalls are discussed later in this chapter.

A six-month-old zoo on its way to five-star fame.

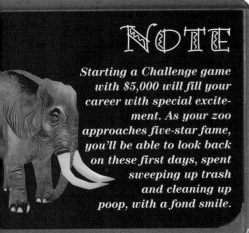

NOTE

Starting a Challenge game with $5,000 will fill your career with special excite- ment. As your zoo approaches five-star fame, you'll be able to look back on these first days, spent sweeping up trash and cleaning up poop, with a fond smile.

SELECTING BIOME TYPE AND MAP SIZE

You should select map size based on three main consid- erations: your experience, the amount of time you want to put into this particular game, and your personal goals for the game. Handling zoo layout correctly on large maps can be difficult for newer players. The placing of exhibits and guest ameni- ties has to be exactly right to draw guests into the farthest corners of your zoo. Chapter 2 has more details on this subject.

Your personal goals will also influence your choice of map size. If you want to exhibit all 30 species in the game, you should choose a medium or large map. If you want to exhibit *and breed* all 30 species, you should choose a large map. Small maps force you to focus on details, such as getting the size of an exhibit exactly right, or placing a guest amenity in the perfect spot. Larger maps allow more leeway with details, but require you to see the larger picture and plan far ahead.

NOTE

Building up a zoo to the max on a large map can take as many as 60 hours of gameplay. If you are not prepared for a big time investment, it's wiser to choose a smaller map.

Selecting biome type is important only if you want to work with the terrain type to create a zoo that looks spectacular from first-person (guest) view. Modifying the terrain in *ZT2* is both easy and free of charge, so transforming an Alpine map into an expanse suitable for an airport takes only a few minutes' work with the Level Terrain brush. However, selecting the biome type assumes extra importance if you're an ambitious tycoon who has chosen to set starting money to $5,000. This is because the amount of money that you can raise by recycling existing zoo objects varies greatly depending on biome type. The list below gives you an idea of what to expect when selecting a *large* map of a given biome type:

- Alpine: a little over $4,000
- Boreal Forest: just over $4,200
- Desert: around $3,600
- Grassland: around $6,000
- Polar Coast: just over $1,100
- River: around $5,000
- Savannah: just over $4,500
- Safari Ridge: just over $2,300
- Scrub: just over $1,000
- Temperate Forest: just over $7,700
- Tropical Rainforest: around $8,000
- Tundra: just over $1,100
- Wetlands: just over $4,200

NOTE

You will get much less money from recycled zoo objects if you play a medium or small map. Games on such maps don't play well with a $5,000 starting budget unless you're making a point of learning more about zoo finances. Since games played on smaller maps are almost always training games, feel free to award yourself more starting money.

Note that you might not want to recycle everything. Most of the time, you'll want to keep at least the initial stretch of the path by the zoo entrance. You'll also want to keep at least some vegetation and rocks that will be useful in finishing exhibits for which you cannot obtain objects because of low zoo fame. For example, choosing a Wetlands biome type will enable you to trick out an early flamingo exhibit with an almost full set of features in spite of low zoo fame. Some biome types contain miscellaneous zoo objects; for instance, the large Wetlands map features some furniture (benches, picnic tables) and a gazebo. The gazebo becomes available only at three-star fame, and benches and picnic tables are useful from the start. Keep an eye out for opportunities like that when recycling!

THE $5,000 CHALLENGE

Playing a $5,000-starting-money Challenge game is the favorite sport of every ambitious tycoon. Bringing your zoo to five-star fame from such humble beginnings will reward you with an extra sense of accomplishment, and confirm you really know how to play the game.

If you want to begin your Challenge game with more money, you'll still find later sections of this walkthrough useful. Unfortunately, the size of this guide does not permit individual walkthroughs for Challenge games started with varying amounts of money. It's hardest to get things going with just $5,000, so the walkthrough accommodates the brave players who have selected that amount.

The sections below will take you through what needs to be done to develop your zoo into a big attraction and a mean money machine. Once you reach this point, you'll be able to pursue whatever strategy appeals to you. Your cash flow will let you afford even expensive mistakes, although you shouldn't be making any of those after reading the preceding chapters!

The walkthrough is based on a game that takes place on a large City Zoo map. This map is the right choice for your first attempt at a five-grand, five-star Challenge game for two reasons: The easy terrain makes it a snap to visualize your future zoo, so zoo layout is easy. At the same time, you get a nice bit of extra money from recycling—maybe not a lot, but it's adequate.

THE OPENING

Preparing your zoo for opening takes a while. You should pause a new game right at the start; if it's a new map, scroll all over it to get the lay of the land. It's a good idea to keep the game paused while you're spending your starting money.

You have to utilize the zoo walls to build a decent-sized exhibit with just $5,000 starting money. Of course, it will also be a sunken exhibit with low fencing, because that gives zoo guests a better view and saves you money (see Chapter 2 for details). Place it to the side of the zoo entrance—not too close, because you want space in the entrance area, and not too far, because you don't want to spend unnecessary money on pathways. Remember to flatten/smooth out the terrain as appropriate before building fences or paths across it, and to recycle any objects that might be in the way!

There are only four animal species to choose from, and just three species available at a time from the animal adoption panel. You definitely want to start your zoo with a camel or moose exhibit. These are the two starting species that are inexpensive to set up, and they use enrichment objects (scratching posts), which lets you complete a lucrative photo challenge at little cost. Overall, the camel is slightly better than the moose as your first zoo species because it requires much less maintenance and can use a shelter to satisfy privacy needs. Its exhibit is also easy to build and inexpensive to upgrade—it's the desert, after all.

TIP

If a camel isn't one of the initial choices on the adoption panel, get your zoo going with a moose. Don't wait to acquire a camel as a replacement for a declined species.

As explained earlier in this guide, you should always build exhibits of decent size that can comfortably accommodate at least four animals of a given species. You can build two such exhibits side by side using the zoo's front wall as the exhibits' back wall. However, you start with enough money for just one. Select the low chain-link fence for maximum economy. After fencing off the exhibit area, proceed to lower the exhibit floor as described in Chapter 2. Paint it with the free biome brushes, and finish by adding dips and rises (or, for the moose, a steep hill and/or a screen of trees that can hide it from view to give it some privacy).

Your next step is to lay out a path leading to the exhibit, and mark out a viewing area. Do it as described in Chapter 2, and put down a donation box. Now adopt a pair of animals, one of each sex, and place them in the exhibit.

Buy a dish of water and a dish with the animals' preferred food as shown in the Zookeeper's Recommendations panel. It's time to unpause the game and/or open your zoo (see Figure 6.4). For now, leave the admission price at Moderate.

FIGURE 6.4:

Here they come!

FIRST GUESTS, FIRST CHALLENGES

Your next step is to provide basic guest amenities. Placing a couple of small restrooms is priority number one; a couple of benches come second. Put down a hot dog stand, a soda stand, and a pretzel cart next, and don't forget to buy at least one trash can at the same time! For the next month or so of game time, you'll act as zookeeper and maintenance worker while watching out for a good photo challenge. The important word here is "good," because taking on some challenges can be a bad move! You'll find more details on that near the end of this chapter and in Appendix C.

At this stage of the game, you're working with one end in mind: to exhibit a new species as quickly as possible. If you've got a camel, go for the moose next; if you've got a moose, get a camel. Extend the front fence of your first exhibit to the zoo's side wall and set up the second exhibit. Lay down a path to it before adopting new animals, and remember that you need to purchase food/water dishes and another donation box, too! Fortunately, adopting a pair of moose or camels costs just $2,500. This is the right moment to recycle remaining zoo objects! You'll be able to afford your new animals fast.

Expect your zoo fame to hit one full star soon after you adopt your second species. Touch up your exhibits with the free biome brushes before spending money on trees, plants, and rocks. The quality of the animal habitats has a big effect on guest donations—they should look as natural as possible to maximize guest entertainment and educational benefits. Add more guest amenities: extra benches, a couple of picnic tables, trash cans, and an extra restroom, followed by the gift cart, which becomes available with one-star fame (no research required). Researching the first guest amusement—a kangaroo bouncy ride—comes next. Although it won't earn back its cost through increased guest donations for a while, it will raise your guests' happiness.

Focus on saving up money for your third exhibit next. Keep in mind that you can rapidly increase both zoo fame and your money by completing photo challenges that reward you with a fame boost and/or a grant. It's even possible to build a third exhibit and purchase a pair of new animals before the end of the game's second month. However, in most games you won't be able to do it until March.

Your fourth animal should be the gemsbok, which becomes available with one-star fame. It's a low-maintenance, inexpensive animal that will help you reach one-and-a-half-star zoo fame quickly—even more quickly if you agree to a fame-boosting challenge, such as acquiring publicity photos for your zoo's marketing department. Placing the fourth exhibit depends on your plans for zoo expansion. Place the exhibit in agreement with the zoo-layout principles discussed in Chapter 2. Remember to make this scrub exhibit big enough to let you add kangaroos later.

Don't forget to invest in research of the new guest amenities and amusements that become available with one-star fame. They help maximize guest happiness, which in turn boosts zoo fame. You want to reach two-star fame as quickly as possible, because it is a significant milestone in the development of your zoo. The family restroom, the compost building, a whole range of new guest amenities, an extra adoption slot on the adoption panel—these are just a few of the new options that open up at two-star fame. Utilizing these options will enable you jump quickly toward the next milestone: three-star fame, which lets you access many exotic vegetation and rock types for zoo exhibits.

TIP

Place a gift cart in front of every exhibit as soon as it becomes available at one-star zoo fame. Gift carts (and, later, also gift shops) not only turn very nice profits, but also make guests happier. Guests like owning souvenirs of their visit to your zoo!

NOTE

If you've quickly brought your first exhibit up to a high standard, you could be rewarded by news of animal pregnancies by February of the first game year. And babies mean more money and more fame for your zoo!

121

Remember that ZT2 lets you remodel exhibits into new habitat types at minimal cost. You'll transfer animals to new exhibits or move them between existing ones quite often when creating a zoo on a medium or large map.

With the four exhibits you've built to date, the amount of money flowing into your donation boxes should increase considerably. You'll be kept increasingly busy taking care of animals and zoo trash. Animal demands grow sharply when babies arrive; fortunately, so do donations, and this is the time when you should hire your first zookeeper and a maintenance worker. Your zoo should be making enough money to let you add a new species every month for the next three months. After that, you should pause your expansion and give each of the newly acquired species a mate. Good animal choices in the one-star to two-star fame range include the zebra (put it in with the Thomson's gazelles to gain a multispecies exhibit), the ibex (inexpensive, breeds quickly and profusely), and the flamingo.

The Road to Savannah

By the time your zoo reaches one-and-a-half-star fame, your adoption choices will include two savannah species: the Thomson's gazelle and the zebra. New savannah species are made available with every extra half-star of fame until your zoo reaches three stars. Building toward creating a big savannah exhibit at the back of the zoo is the best strategy you can adopt now that your zoo is producing enough income to build the needed financial muscle.

Continue adding exhibits along the zoo's side wall. The gemsbok exhibit should have been the first of these side-wall exhibits; add an ibex and an emperor penguin next. These two will bring you close enough to the zoo's back wall to begin work on your big savannah exhibit. Initially, build an exhibit to hold the zebras and gazelles available. For layout purposes, it's simplest to build almost a mirror image of the two exhibits that lie along the zoo's front wall. The only differences will be that your savannah exhibit should be deeper by six to 10 tiles, and that being a single exhibit, it won't have the fence in the middle. Now all you need is to lay a path from the entrance to the corner of your new savannah exhibit, and you will have completed the first of the two grand loops of your zoo highway system. Remember that you'll be expanding the savannah exhibit later, and don't run the path all the way to the back wall! If you find yourself in a design dilemma, turn to Chapter 2 for help.

Don't neglect to research some animal toys, or enrichment objects. They satisfy the animals' Stimulation needs, and make watching guests feel entertained. However, don't get carried away by all the nice new research options. Don't research anything that you don't need or that you won't build right away! It's a waste of time and money.

Move the gazelles and the zebras to the new savannah exhibit. The old, medium-sized exhibit can be remodeled into a tundra exhibit for penguins. Penguins don't use a man-made shelter and are sociable animals; the extra size of the exhibit will let you provide enough privacy for numerous birds, even though no trees are available for the tundra biome.

By this point in the game, you'll have had many new animal births. Consider releasing a couple of the older specimens into the wild; it will reduce the pressure on your zookeeper and yourself, letting you delay hiring extra staff. The boost in zoo fame for releasing animals into the wild will compensate for any drop caused by a lower number of animals in your zoo. You might also be forced into letting some of the animals go because your superior care has made them multiply very rapidly.

If you are very successful at breeding animals, you may have to deal with sudden overcrowding in one of the exhibits. Overcrowded animals cannot be released into the wild; to solve this quandary, crate some of the animals you'll keep, and move them out of the exhibit. Release one or more of the animals remaining in the exhibit, then let the crated animals back inside. Note that you can always put up an animal for adoption, even if its needs aren't fully satisfied.

Reaching the back wall of your zoo necessitates the building of a new guest service center in that area. Start humbly with a family restroom and a single food stand, a drink stand, and a guest amusement. Leave plenty of space for future additions! Remember that the rear half of your zoo will contain exhibits with many species, or exotic species. It's the only way to ensure good traffic flow to the rear of your zoo. Once you have that, you'll get plenty of thirsty and hungry guests far away from your first guest service area.

You should be able to begin work on the big savannah exhibit around the end of your first year. The exact timing depends on the amount of luck you've had with photo challenges, especially in the first few months of the game, when an extra couple of grand can make a huge difference. Your zoo fame should be around three and a half stars. Remember, the number of animals you've released to the wild also plays a role!

TAKING CARE OF GUESTS

In the meantime, don't forget to take good care of your guests! Your construction effort should be split between building new exhibits and building guest amenities. As your zoo's fame increases, more and more guests enter expecting fulfillment of all their needs.

During the first three months of the game, focus on developing a guest area that will service the front half of your zoo. Mark off a dedicated guest service area with a path as soon as you've completed exhibit number three. Then begin researching new buildings and structures. It's safest to start with a hamburger stand and a water drink stand; once you've got them, research a couple of guest-amusement and decorative structures such as gorilla climbing bars or an elephant fountain. Don't forget to make the guest service area aesthetically pleasing (see Figure 6.5). Refer to Chapter 3 for more details.

TIP

Exchange all small restrooms for the new family model as soon as it becomes available (with two-star zoo fame). The family restroom is vastly more efficient, and there's no research involved. There are no excuses! Treat your guests to the ultimate lavatory experience.

FIGURE 6.5:

Even a few trees can make things look much better.

Once you've built your big savannah exhibit, turn your attention to developing another guest service area in the back half of your zoo. Then follow the advice in Chapter 2 and "fill in" the first complete loop of your zoo highway system with new exhibits, decorations, extra guest amenities, etc.

While adding new guest amenities, remember the all-important rule: guests will be happy only if the animals are happy. Do not skimp on hiring zookeepers because you want that restaurant first; do not postpone researching new animal toys and retouching the exhibits with new foliage because you want money for a fancy fountain. Veterans of the original *Zoo Tycoon* have to take special care—they'll be tempted to attach too much importance to guest amenities because of their exalted status in the older game.

REACHING FOR FIVE-STAR FAME

You'll need to build many new exhibits before your zoo's fame reaches five stars. It's best to capitalize yet again on the unique benefits of building a multispecies exhibit. There are three extra-large multispecies exhibits: savannah, tropical forest, and wetlands. There are also some slightly smaller ones, such as scrub and temperate forest. In terms of attraction, the savannah, the tropical forest, and the temperate forest rule over the others. The savannah contains the most species, from gazelles to elephants; the tropical forest has entertaining chimps and gorillas in addition to lemurs and okapi; and the temperate forest contains the pandas. Put the tropical rainforest exhibit next to the savannah; these two work well together. Okapi are still relatively inexpensive, and you can get its exhibit going quickly.

Your zoo fame will be hovering around four stars (give or take a half-star) for a long time in the middle to late game. To stabilize your fame level and begin the push for five stars, you'll have to include several exotic species, plus

> **NOTE**
>
> *Guests greatly appreciate meticulously re-created biomes, and every dollar spent on plants, rocks, and trees is almost instantly refunded into the donation box. Your success is shown by the educational smileys that appear over guests viewing a well-appointed exhibit.*

> **TIP**
>
> *Your five-star zoo will need a couple of restaurants. The family restaurant that becomes an option at three-star fame will round off your front guest service area nicely; the fancier type of restaurant available at four-star fame fits well into the back guest service area. Remember to locate the more sophisticated and expensive guest amenities and amusements in the back guest service area. They'll help attract traffic to the farthest reaches of your zoo. Add extra donation boxes in high-traffic areas when your zoo grows beyond three-star fame.*

conduct a review and retouching of all the animal habitats—you'll be seeking to achieve maximum educational impact on zoo guests. You'll also have to acquire new animal toys, and hire extra zookeepers to ensure constant high levels of animal happiness. Once elephants and rhinos arrive in your big savannah exhibit, it will require two zookeepers all by itself—and even then, you'll have to make a personal intervention occasionally.

Note that playing certain Campaign scenarios will improve your Challenge-game skills. The special stand-alone scenario, the Mysterious Panda, plus a couple of others are very much like Challenge games without the photo-safari and game challenges! Refer to Chapter 7 for details, and don't forget about the extra advice and tips on zoo development in Chapters 2 through 5.

PHOTO-SAFARI CHALLENGES

TIP

There is one in-game challenge that's a killer. It consists of a loan offer: $10,000 with 20% interest and an indefinite repayment term. The catch is that you lose 40% of your income until you repay $12,000. This can cripple initial zoo development and leave you twiddling your thumbs for months on end. There is no advantage in taking on this challenge under any circumstances.

A Challenge game includes numerous photo-safari and game challenges. These often represent opportunities to have fun with the game's camera mode. Most often, a challenge is a chance to make extra money and/or increase zoo fame. Some challenges may see you break even or lose a little financially, but the increase in fame and monthly zoo income is clearly worth it. But sometimes, a challenge will bring you nothing but sorrow. Read the challenge text carefully and make sure you understand its implications! If you agree to photograph an animal using an enrichment object, but no species in your zoo uses *any* enrichment objects, you'll have to get yourself a new species before you can take that picture—or you'll have to decline the challenge.

As mentioned earlier, you'll find a complete list of challenges in Appendix C. However, some general comments apply across the board. You should always consider the ease of completing a challenge first. New challenges are offered periodically throughout the game; if you aren't currently engaged in one, you'll be offered a new one every month. If you decline, another challenge will be offered in its place after a short delay. Remember that most challenges can be completed only once, and sooner or later you'll be faced with those you've previously chosen to avoid.

Read the list of challenges in Appendix C to preview all the choices on offer. Some challenges, such as the Alfred Windsor Photography Award, are transparently easy and bring quick rewards (see Figure 6.6)—if you adopt animals in pairs, you won't have a problem photographing two together! Several easy challenges increase zoo fame, but when they don't also carry financial rewards, you might want to think twice. Higher zoo fame means greater guest expectations, and in the opening months of the game, you need money first and foremost; fame almost takes care of itself in the early stages of a Challenge game.

NOTE

Challenges that require you to photograph a specific animal activity can be tricky. You might be asked to photograph a moose rubbing its antlers against a tree, for example. It's not easy to figure out what your moose are up to in the trees, so watch the animal's Current Activity shown under the Animal status tab on the animal's info panel.

FIGURE 6.6:

The Alfred Windsor Photography Award is often the first award you'll win in a Challenge game.

In summary, when a challenge is relatively easy, check if you can make a monetary profit. If not, think twice and consider your circumstances carefully before acceptance.

Snapping the Right Picture

Once you've decided to accept a challenge, the way you go about executing it may greatly increase your chances of capturing the needed shots. Things are simple if you're required to photograph an inanimate object such as a tree, but they get tricky when you're asked to photograph a zoo event. Do not stroll around in camera view, hoping to see what you need to photograph! Instead, follow these guidelines:

1. Identify where the event is likely to take place, then hover over that area in overhead view, close enough to see clearly what's going on.

2. Once an event is looking likely, zoom in while still in overhead view to put yourself above the spot from which you'll take the photograph.

3. Switch to camera mode and take the required picture.

TIP

Sometimes you can hit two ... um ...rubber ducks with one stone. If you can capture two required events in one picture, more power to you. For example, snapping a guest drinking a soda while seated on a bench completes the Marketing Department photo challenge (which asks for pictures of a guest sitting and of a guest drinking a soda).

ZOO TYCOON 2 FEATURES A CAMPAIGN GAME THAT'S SOMEWHAT UNIQUE. THE SCENARIOS ARE GROUPED INTO SIX CAMPAIGNS, THE LAST OF WHICH IS CALLED THE MYSTERIOUS PANDA AND CAN BE UNLOCKED ONLY BY FINISHING THE CONSERVATION PROGRAMS CAMPAIGN. COMPLETING ALL THE OTHER CAMPAIGNS, WHICH YOU CAN DO IN ANY ORDER, UNLOCKS A DECORATIVE ZOO OBJECT THAT CAN BE USED IN ALL THE GAMES YOU PLAY—CAMPAIGN, FREEFORM, AND CHALLENGE.

THIS CHAPTER PROVIDES YOU WITH WALKTHROUGHS OF ALL THE SCENARIOS IN ALL OF THE CAMPAIGNS. TO MAKE REFER-ENCING INDIVIDUAL WALKTHROUGHS EASIER FOR YOU, THE CAMPAIGNS AND THE SCENARIOS WITHIN ARE DISCUSSED IN THE SAME ORDER AS THEY ARE PRESENTED ON THE ZT2 CAMPAIGN-GAME MENU. THIS DOES NOT MEAN YOU SHOULD PLAY THE CAMPAIGNS AND THE SCENARIOS IN THAT EXACT ORDER. WHEN YOU COMPLETE THE ZOOKEEPER IN TRAINING CAMPAIGN, IT'S NOT A BAD IDEA TO CHOOSE CONSERVATION PROGRAMS NEXT, AND THEN PROGRESS TO TROUBLED ZOOS. COMPLETING THESE THREE CAMPAIGNS WILL SHARPEN YOUR TYCOON SKILLS NICELY, AND GET YOU READY FOR THE MORE SEVERE TESTS CONTAINED IN THE REMAINING SCENARIOS OF

CAMPAIGN WALKTHROUGHS

The sections that follow contain walkthroughs for all the scenarios in the *ZT2* campaign, tutorial excepted. The *ZT2* tutorial is self-explanatory—it's a tutorial after all. You'll find a couple of tutorial comments at the end of Chapter 1.

Remember that the walkthroughs aren't the only way to play and win a given scenario. It's your game, and you should use your imagination when you play—you just might come up with the ultimate strategy! Also, the walkthroughs do not include detailed instructions on how to build a particular exhibit or care for a given animal unless it is of particular importance in a scenario. All general zoo information, data, and tips are included in Chapters 2 through 5, and the appendices at the end of this guide.

One important point: to simplify giving directions, all walkthroughs assume that you are viewing your zoo as it appears on the Overview Map.

ZOOKEEPER IN TRAINING

Predictably, this is the easiest campaign, and it's the recommended starting point for all players. It's a good idea to complete all scenarios in a given campaign before moving on to another, particularly if you're new to *Zoo Tycoon*. Completing all three scenarios in this campaign unlocks the flowerpost.

NEW ANIMAL ARRIVALS

Difficulty: Easy
Map: Grassland, small
Starting Cash: $30,000
Goals:

🖐 Place a hippo, a lion, and a polar bear in appropriate exhibits.

🖐 Satisfy the animals' needs for a month.

WALKTHROUGH

This scenario is really a continuation of the tutorial. Winning it takes about two minutes. That's how long it will take you to place each of the three animals in the appropriate exhibit together with a dish of water and suitable food. The hippo goes into the wetlands exhibit (farthest from the zoo entrance), the lion into the savannah exhibit (between wetlands and the zoo entrance), the polar bear into the tundra exhibit (to the right of the zoo entrance). Then open the zoo to the public and watch them come!

A full month must pass before the scenario is declared as won, and in that time, you can do one of three things. The first approach is to spend most of the month in first-person view, strolling around your zoo, taking care of the animals, possibly shooting a roll of film. The second approach is to build an extra exhibit, some guest amenities, and *then* stroll around, taking care of animals as necessary. The enclosed area beside the zoo entrance is perfect for an exhibit (see Figure 7.1); it already has a zookeeper's gate, and all you need to do is replace the solid concrete fencing with a fence type that will let guests view the animals inside.

Put a donation box in a strategic spot by each exhibit! It should be the very first thing you do once you've put each of the three starting animals where it belongs. Acquire the proper tycoon reflexes right at the start, and you won't have to remember so many things later.

FIGURE 7.1:

Your little zoo can hit one-star fame before the month is over.

The third approach involves spending all of your starting money wisely to build three new exhibits for all three animals initially available in the animal-adoption panel, plus guest amenities. There's enough space, and there's enough money if you don't waste any! If you go that route, you'll have to hire a zookeeper and a maintenance worker before you have the freedom and the time to stroll around.

START-UP ZOO

Difficulty: Easy
Map: Grassland, small
Starting Cash: $30,000
Goals:

- Create an exhibit for a pair of zebras.

- Build a hot dog stand and a soda stand.

- Photograph a zebra running, and photograph a zebra using a scratching post (prior research needed).

- Create an exhibit for a pair of jaguars and satisfy all their needs for a month.

WALKTHROUGH

TIP

You can save $175 on a water dish if you place a little puddle in the exhibit; the animals will drink from it.

This scenario can be noticeably harder than the preceding one. Mainly, this is due to the challenge of photographing a zebra when it's rubbing against a scratching post, but you'll find a tip on how to deal with that later in this walkthrough.

There's an octagonal grassland exhibit ready and waiting for you when you start the scenario. Recycle all the objects inside the exhibit, and paint it with the savannah brush. Remember to employ the full savannah palette, but don't plant any trees! You don't need to include shallow water, either. However, do include some extra plants and make a point of placing several rocks.

Place the zebras inside the exhibit together with food and water—do not hire a zookeeper! Immediately begin researching the scratching post. While waiting for research results, build the required hot dog stand and soda stand atop the paved area with picnic tables; it's located behind the zebra exhibit. If you really want to do things right, move the whole guest amenity area in *front* of the zebra exhibit; its default location is poor. However, for the purposes of winning this scenario, you can leave zoo layout as is. Just add an extra small restroom and a couple of benches—you've got plenty of cash.

Your next goal is to take two pictures of zebra activities: running, and rubbing against a scratching post. Put down the scratching post in a central location—this lets you take a picture from any angle. Make sure your zebras are happy enough to prance about by personally taking care of all their needs *except* hygiene. If you tried being clever and hired a zookeeper against the solemn advice in this walkthrough, you'll now be punished by the zookeeper intervening to keep the zebras clean. Your plans may also be rendered null and void by the presence of trees. The big secret is this: zebras rub against something when they itch, and they itch when they're slightly dirty. If there's a tree available, they most often rub against it (see Figure 7.2).

NOTE

Don't try to pack the jaguars into the tiny steel-bar enclosure where the crates with the animals are deposited! It's far too small. You can expand it, of course, but a clever tycoon will just recycle the expensive steel-bar fencing and build an exhibit from scratch.

FIGURE 7.2:

Get rid of the trees in the zebra exhibit to see some scratching-post action.

Make sure you give your zebras a nice big rubdown once you've got the scratching-post picture—they'll need it! If they haven't previously been happy enough to run around, they will be now. When you've got both zebra pictures, you'll be given a new assignment: to build a comfortable exhibit for a pair of jaguars that has been just deposited by the front entrance. It's a good idea to build it to the side of the guest service area if you left it as is: the jaguars' presence nearby will encourage guest traffic and boost sales revenues. This doesn't really matter in this scenario, but the ambitious tycoon spares no effort to improve his skills. Of course, you may put the jaguar exhibit elsewhere—

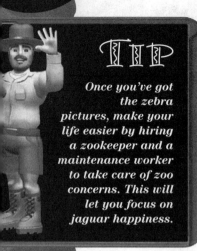

beside the front entrance, for example. But wherever you put it, don't forget to put down a donation box right after you've laid out the viewing area!

The big catch in keeping the jaguars happy for a month is this: your zoo fame is too low to let you purchase any tropical rainforest trees, and jaguars like trees. The best you can do is build a nice, big exhibit complete with a pond (jaguars like water) and a choice of food (both meat and fish). Use every tropical rainforest brush in selected areas to create a relatively balanced biome in spite of the absence of trees and rocks. Make sure the jaguars have individual small wooden shelters, and several enrichment objects—research a ball in addition to the scratching post, and buy a beef shank. Finally, make sure the big cats stay clean—they arrive already slightly soiled. If you stay on your toes, you will have no trouble keeping the jaguars content until the month ends, even though the exhibit has no trees.

BEYOND START-UP

Difficulty: Normal
Map: Grassland, medium
Starting Cash: $30,000
Goal:

Starting from scratch, collect $5,000 in guest donations.

WALKTHROUGH

This scenario will be a walkover for players who completed a few Challenge games prior to playing the campaign. Although there is an absence of photo challenges, the game goals are the same: build a nice zoo, make money.

The $30,000 starting money is sufficient to build four exhibits and guest amenities right away. However, you should begin by recycling most of the zoo's existing path: it's an insult to economical and effective zoo layout. You should go for the butterfly opening; two sets of two exhibits each, one on each side of the central path and guest service area—just like a butterfly's wings and body (see Figure 7.3).

FIGURE 7.3:
The final scenario of the Zookeeper in Training campaign tests your zoo-layout skills.

Start by building two exhibits, one on each side of the zoo entrance, and utilizing the zoo walls. It's best to kick things off with a camel and a moose, just like in a Challenge game, but Thomson's gazelles will do nicely, too. You'll be building a third exhibit very shortly anyway. Set zoo admission to Free and open the zoo to the public as soon as you've completed the first two exhibits, adopted animals, laid down the paths, and placed the donation boxes. You need to collect $5,000 in donations to win this scenario, and you might as well start right away.

While the first guests are coming in, build the available guest amenities: *two* small restrooms, a hot dog stand, a soda stand, a pretzel cart, benches, a few picnic tables. Spare no expense when making guests happy, because higher guest happiness means more money in the donation boxes. You should be getting messages that guests love your zoo shortly after completing your third exhibit. It's quite possible to glide to victory on three exhibits—moose, camel, and Thomson's gazelle. However, every serious tycoon should complete the butterfly layout with a fourth exhibit. At this point, you'll be able to afford either the common peafowl or the emperor

> **NOTE**
>
> *There is no need to hire a zookeeper or a maintenance worker in this scenario, but astute tycoons will be able to afford it. You'll also be able to afford male/female pairs of animals of each species. This is always the optimal way to add a new species to your zoo, boosting the flow of guest donations considerably.*

penguin. You'll easily raise sufficient cash by recycling the remaining starting zoo objects, because by now there'll be a stream of dollars coming into your donation boxes. Expect to hit the $5,000 target in the second month of the scenario (February).

TROUBLED ZOOS

This campaign is all about fixing zoos. All three scenarios see you taking over a zoo on the edge of disaster, and quickly transforming it into a model facility. In other words, this campaign tests your problem-solving skills, so necessary for every tycoon that aspires to five-star fame. Troubled Zoos is best played as either the second or third campaign in the *ZT2* Campaign game, after Zookeeper in Training and (optionally) Conservation Programs.

Completing all three scenarios in the Troubled Zoos campaign unlocks the flower arch.

WALTHAM ANIMAL PARK REDEVELOPMENT EFFORT

Difficulty: Normal
Map: Grassland, medium
Starting Cash: $10,000
Goals:

- Hire two maintenance workers and two zookeepers.
- Clean up the zoo.
- Ensure that the basic needs of all zoo animals are met.
- Enhance animal exhibits.
- Place donation boxes.
- Adopt one new animal.
- Meet the Privacy needs of all animals in the zoo.

WALKTHROUGH

This scenario begins on an interesting note: the zoo is closed, and closed it will remain until you've fulfilled the first set of goals. Once you've done that, you'll be asked to adopt a new animal and meet the Privacy needs of all animals in the zoo. The new requests are accompanied by a $5,000 grant, which ensures you have enough dollars to spend on animal shelters, and tweaks to an animal habitat if you adopted a moose as the required new animal. As you already know from previous chapters, the moose has no use for man-made shelters, and must seek privacy behind habitat features such as trees and hills.

When the scenario starts, the zoo is a mess and the animals are dirty and unhappy. Instantly hire the four zoo personnel specified in the scenario goal, then help zookeepers deal with the unhappy animals. It's best to put one zookeeper with the zebras and the other with the elephant while you parachute down into the Bengal tiger's exhibit to groom and heal the big cat (see Figure 7.4). Proceed to clean the tiger's exhibit and replenish its food and water; then build a shelter and run over to help out your zookeepers. Build a shelter in the zebra exhibit, and touch up the habitat with the savannah brush, adding trees, plants, and rocks as appropriate. Repeat the process in the elephant's exhibit—note that you cannot build a shelter there. It doesn't matter, because the elephant's Privacy need is satisfied when the scenario starts, and there are no zoo guests. The zebra and elephant exhibits have patches of grassland that need to be painted over with a savannah biome brush, while the Bengal tiger's needs more grass and a small pond.

FIGURE 7.4:

The sick Bengal tiger needs to be healed quickly.

You most likely won't need to help out your maintenance workers. Place a donation box by each exhibit next, and patrol for trash only if you aren't given the new scenario goals—the zoo must be clean before you can receive a new set of scenario goals and $5,000.

Fiddle with the animal choices in the adoption panel until you obtain the Thomson's gazelle. It's a savannah species, which means you can simply drop the new animal into one of the two existing savannah exhibits. However, you also have enough cash to build a completely new exhibit (the camel exhibit is easiest), should you so desire.

Within a short time, the zebras and the tiger will have rested in their respective shelters, and you'll hear that all the animals' Privacy needs have been satisfied. This wins you the scenario.

RAINTREE COOPERATIVE ANIMAL PARK

Difficulty: Normal
Map: Tropical Rainforest, small
Starting Cash: $5,000
Goal:

 Make existing zoo exhibits suitable for zoo animals.

WALKTHROUGH

It's a good idea to switch to the Overview Map at the start of the scenario. It gives you a clear picture of what's located where in your zoo.

This scenario tests the financial acumen of all incipient tycoons. If you think the way a true tycoon thinks, you'll win this scenario almost the moment you unpause the game. Yes, the very first thing you should do in this scenario is pause it (unless you want to truly challenge your tycoon skills). Then have a look around. It's very enlightening: the Raintree Cooperative Animal Park is a perfect example of how you should *not* build a zoo. There are plenty of items meant to pamper nonexistent guests, but the animal exhibits are a horror show.

Being a true tycoon, you know what counts most is the happiness of the animals. You don't have enough cash to make all the animals in your zoo happy, so start recycling. The zoo features a very nice bit of decorative fencing that's of no use to anybody (there are no guests to view it), plus a guest service area at the very end of the main path. Recycle the food and drink stands, the picnic tables, the lampposts, and the flowerbeds by the path, and finally also the trees, rocks, and plants in the zoo. You might as well recycle most of the fencing from the exhibits that initially contain the zoo animals. Just leave short stretches of fencing by the path for future building reference. All these smooth moves will result in more than tripling your starting money. You will have over $15,000—more than enough to make all animals comfortable.

Begin by stretching existing fencing along the path, then proceed to build four big rectangular exhibits as shown in Figure 7.5. Then model the habitats with loving care, with the game still paused. Note that most of the animals' food and water is gone (only the moose is relatively well supplied).

FIGURE 7.5:
Rebuilding the zoo exhibits is a snap given all the money from recycling.

You'll have tons of money left after spending all you can on the exhibits, unless you waste a truly prodigious amount. Make your new exhibits more elegant by relocating (selling, then building anew) all animal shelters to the rear of the exhibits.

If you've done a good job on the animal exhibits, you don't even need to put zookeeper gates into the exhibit fencing. Unpause the game and race through all four exhibits by yourself,

NOTE

If you intend to continue playing this scenario after you've won it, build a nice little guest service area in front of the camel exhibit. You can easily afford to hire a zookeeper or a maintenance worker right away, too.

replenishing food and drink, grooming the animals, and cleaning the exhibit as appropriate. If you're a lazy tycoon, you'll be able to hire four zookeepers easily, and put one in each exhibit to begin with. You'll receive the news you've won the scenario shortly after unpausing the game.

WOLVERTON ANIMAL REHABILITATION CENTER

Difficulty: Normal
Map: Boreal Forest, small
Starting Cash: $5,000
Goals:

- Heal zoo animals and satisfy their needs.

- Reach three-star fame.

WALKTHROUGH

This is by far the toughest of the scenarios discussed so far in this chapter. The big problem is the existing zoo layout. Since so many things are in place when you start, tearing up everything and building the zoo from scratch while animals are crated isn't an attractive option. However, there's a lot of recycling and rebuilding to be done the moment the scenario starts, even when you stick with the existing zoo setup.

Begin by pausing the game and taking a good look at the Overview Map. Jump to the zebra and moose exhibits, and begin by reconstructing those; they need expanding for future additions such as baby animals or other species from the same biome. You'll notice that all exhibits in this scenario have very expensive fencing. Replacing that fencing with chain link lets you greatly

FIGURE 7.6:

Make sure the zebras' savannah exhibit is large enough to accommodate another four or five animals.

expand the exhibits *and* make money in the process. Begin by expanding the zebra exhibit; you can even afford to use slightly pricier wooden bar fencing, as shown in Figure 7.6. Recycling a section of the original concrete fencing brings in $120, while a section of chain link or wooden bar fencing costs $75 or $90 respectively. You'll be adding Thomson's gazelles to this exhibit, and there will be baby animals appearing on the scene, too, so don't skimp on space!

Give the moose exhibit a makeover next, replacing the fencing and at least doubling the exhibit area. You may have to modify the terrain a little before expanding the exhibit. The beaver exhibit across the path from the moose can be left as is, but don't forget to recycle the post-and-rope fence that runs from the beaver exhibit to the zoo entrance. It's worth $1,000 and performs no useful role.

Spend some time working with the Flatten Terrain brush to level things out; the scenario zoo has been built on Boreal Forest terrain with little or no preparation. Terrain that's too steep for fencing or paths is shaded yellow; use the Smooth Terrain brush to even things out. Refer to Chapter 2 for more construction-work details.

TIP

This scenario requires you to make some terrain modifications inside the animals' exhibits. Flatten the terrain in the zebras' exhibit, and build a screen of trees or a hill for the moose to hide behind when it needs privacy.

You'll also want to clean up the path layout and rearrange the movable zoo objects a little. There are several bottlenecks in the path network; they're easy to locate—in several places, the pathway narrows down to single tile in an important spot. Clean up the path network and relocate the donation boxes as appropriate, because their initial placing isn't very good. As you remember from previous chapters, the perfect spot for a donation box is where it doesn't obstruct traffic *and* it is passed by all the zoo guests viewing the adjacent exhibit.

You might also want to expand the grizzly-bear exhibit, using the same approach as earlier. If you're running short on money, recycle zoo vegetation and rocks; stick to chain-link fencing if you're afraid of wasting some money during zoo reconstruction. Finally, don't forget to place some extra trash cans and a couple of small restrooms; the single restroom your zoo starts with is woefully inadequate.

You should have enough money left to hire a zookeeper comfortably; I was able to hire *two*, and a maintenance worker as well. Then set the zoo admission to Free, and open your zoo. If you've hired one zookeeper, put him in with the zebras; if two, put the other one with the bears. Tend to the beaver and the moose yourself, replenishing food and water, grooming the animals, and cleaning their exhibits. Continue to tweak zoo layout and the animals' exhibits as your money machine wakes up. You should hit full one-star fame before January is over, and see a steady growth of zoo cash even while paying for two zookeepers and a maintenance worker.

Turn your attention to the animal-adoption panel and make sure the Thomson's gazelle is an option; decline other species if the gazelle isn't immediately available. You should have the $2,500 to purchase a pair very shortly. Put them in together with the zebras. Monitor the zoo, making adjustments as needed, and research items necessary for higher guest and animal happiness—guest-amusement objects such as the kangaroo bouncy ride, and animal toys (enrichment objects). Make sure that every animal that can use a man-made shelter has one in its exhibit!

Even though you've been spending money on research and new toys for animals and people, you should still see a steady increase in zoo cash. Once you've bought a few guest and animal toys, stop spending temporarily to quickly save up cash for a new exhibit. There's a good spot to the side of the zoo entrance, behind the gazebo the scenario starts with. Do keep the gazebo—it's popular with zoo guests and helps satisfy their need to rest! Flatten the terrain behind it, then build an exhibit for camels (see Figure 7.7). Work on it as money allows; you should be able to finish it and adopt a pair of camels by April.

FIGURE 7.7:

A camel exhibit to the side of the zoo entrance will give a strong boost to your zoo's fame.

Check the Zoo Fame panel to see how each aspect of your zoo contributes to zoo fame. Concentrate on maxing out guest and animal happiness at this point; you may also release an animal or two into the wild—it boosts zoo fame nicely. Given your excellent work on the exhibits earlier on, there's sure to be many baby animals around, and you can set free some older specimens! Research and acquire the ice cream cart plus a few guest-amusement and decorative objects (gorilla climbing bars, hippo bouncy ride, elephant fountain). Make sure every animal that can use an enrichment object has one or more available! By tweaking your existing zoo to perfection, you should hit three-star fame without adding extra species. If you do add new species, add male/female pairs and consider expanding existing exhibits to add new biome-compatible species instead of building a new exhibit from scratch. For example, you can expand the beaver exhibit to add flamingoes.

It's possible to hit three-star fame by the end of April if you try hard; more likely, you'll reach it in May, especially if you've hired two zookeepers—the extra expense in staff salaries does slow down expansion a little, but saves a headache.

> ## TIP
>
> *Do not forget to replace the small restrooms with family restrooms as soon as the luxury model becomes available! The family can plays a crucial role in achieving the highest possible levels of guest happiness in this scenario.*

PREVENT ANIMAL ABUSE

This campaign is best played as the fourth in the *ZT2* Campaign game—after Zookeeper in Training, Conservation Programs, and Troubled Zoos. Its three scenarios focus on testing your zoo-layout, financial, and animal-care skills. They are good all-around training before you tackle the toughest campaign— The Globe.

Completing the Prevent Animal Abuse campaign unlocks the sundial.

AFRICAN ELEPHANT RESCUE

Difficulty: Easy
Map: Temperate Forest, small
Starting Cash: $10,000
Goals:

🐾 Create an appropriate exhibit for at least four elephants.

🐾 Satisfy the basic needs of the elephants for three months.

WALKTHROUGH

This interesting scenario charges you with constructing a big elephant exhibit, and subsequently keeping the elephants healthy for three months. You receive just one female elephant to begin with; its approval of your savannah exhibit results in the delivery of another three elephants.

Pause the scenario at the start and locate the area suitable for your elephant exhibit—it's at the back of the zoo, between the guest service area and the zoo's back wall. Recycle everything in that area, including the solid wood fencing lining the pathways. Remember the exhibit has to be extra large! You'll have to do a few tweaks to the pathways, as well, to nicely line up the viewing area with the elephant exhibit—see Figure 7.8.

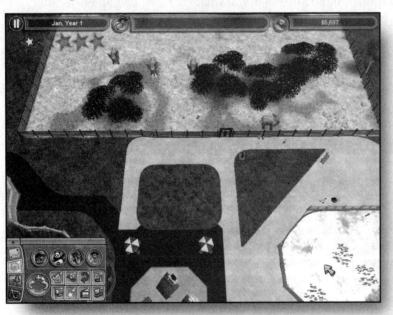

FIGURE 7.8:
You'll have to do some demolition work to comfortably fit in the big elephant exhibit.

Model a savannah habitat inside the exhibit, and when it's ready, move the crated elephant into the enclosure. Don't forget to put in food and water! Follow the elephant tips in Chapter 5 in the unlikely event that you have difficulty making the exhibit suitable. You should receive news of three more elephant arrivals within seconds of unpausing the game with the first elephant inside the new exhibit.

Move the three newly arrived elephants into the big savannah exhibit—it's a good idea to place two water dishes and three food dishes inside. Although the scenario calls for satisfying only the basic needs of these huge animals, you should aim to satisfy their advanced needs as well. It's possible, even though you'll be handicapped by unavailability of items such as an elephant shelter.

Begin by washing the elephants—note that this species needs to be washed often. Don't forget to place many (a half-dozen at least) apples in the exhibit—they're the only enrichment objects available for these animals at this time. Set up a shade shelter as well as a little valley behind a screen of trees so that the animals can get needed privacy.

Attend to the rest of your zoo before you set about making the elephants ecstatically happy. Assign the two zookeepers to exhibits—one should handle the big savannah exhibit and the big wetlands exhibit; the other should help out with the wetlands exhibit and handle the remaining two (polar bear, kangaroos).

Monitor the elephant situation vigilantly while working on zoo fame. You need to increase zoo fame to get access to a pursuit ball, which is much better for keeping elephants entertained than the apples are. Build guest amenities, researching new ones as appropriate. As usual, the kangaroo bouncy ride is mandatory to start with; don't forget to place extra trash cans, a couple of small restrooms (to be replaced with family models as soon as possible), and at least one gift cart—it will be available quickly, because your zoo fame will hit a full star almost immediately. You can also boost fame slightly by releasing a kangaroo into the wild; there are five of them, and you'll be receiving news of assorted animal pregnancies by February anyway.

Your zoo should hit two-star fame before the end of February. Research and buy the pursuit ball for the elephants. If you've designed the exhibit right, satisfying their need of privacy, you'll find that your elephants are one happy bunch of animals. You'll still have to wait until the first days of March for confirmation of your victory; use this time to tweak your zoo layout, adding benches, picnic tables, and trash cans as necessary, and maybe even stroll around and take a few pictures! Do drop in on the elephants a couple of times to ensure all their needs continue to be met.

TIP

Don't forget to include a pond in the savannah exhibit. Elephants love spraying water!

NOTE

Remember the other animals in your zoo! Use the Quick Stats panel to check their status.

COMBATTING CRUELTY

Difficulty: Normal
Map: Grassland, small
Starting Cash: $7,500
Goals:

🐾 Create suitable, separate exhibits for six zebras and eight lions.

🐾 Heal and satisfy basic needs of the lions and the zebras.

🐾 Create a suitable exhibit for seven chimpanzees.

🐾 Heal and satisfy the basic needs of the chimpanzees.

WALKTHROUGH

This scenario tests your skill at fitting three big exhibits into a somewhat cramped zoo layout. The money situation is good if you utilize your tycoon skills and deftly recycle whatever's not necessary.

When you begin, the 14 crates containing the sick animals are ready and waiting. Pause the game to get acquainted with the zoo layout—as usual, begin by switching to the Overview Map. You need to build two very big exhibits, and you'll quickly see that the best choice is the area to the left of the zoo entrance. You'll have to clear the terrain first, and that includes the pretty paved area meant to accommodate food and drink stands. You should also recycle unnecessary pathways, simplifying the path network without any major new path-laying.

Recycling the paved guest service area, the vegetation, and the rocks will bring in a pretty penny—enough to build the two big exhibits required for the zebras and the lions (naturally, the eight lions need a bigger exhibit than the six zebras). Proceed to flatten the terrain in the construction area prior to building, as recommended in Chapter 2, then build the fences needed for both exhibits as shown in Figure 7.9. Making use of the zoo walls and having the two exhibits share a fence will save you lots of money; you can even afford wooden bar fencing for the zebras if that's your fancy. Animals are sensitive to environment outside their exhibits, so putting two savannah exhibits side by side will make your lions and zebras feel even better. You didn't forget to place donation boxes, right?

Spend some more time raising extra funds by trimming a pathway here and recycling a couple of trees there, and you'll easily be able to afford the standard starting guest-service setup: a couple of small restrooms, hot dog and soda stands, some benches, picnic tables, and trash cans. The area in front of the big mountain in the center of the zoo is perfect for setting up guest amenities.

FIGURE 7.9:
You need to modify the existing path network to build the two big exhibits.

What follows is the rather laborious transfer of all the animal crates into the appropriate exhibits. Do not uncrate both sets of animals at the same time! The correct procedure is as follows: first, place *several* water and food dishes in each exhibit—all those animals are pretty hungry and thirsty, and you don't want them to wait too long. Then uncrate one set of animals—it doesn't matter which one—and immediately step inside their exhibit, landing next to the food and water dishes. Groom and heal each animal as it approaches to eat; if you stand in the right spot, all the animals will pass right by you. Repeat the procedure for the second set of animals. If your healing efforts seem to fail, switch to Overhead View to pick up the animal concerned, and put it in front of the food and water. This should end the animal's melancholic mindset and let it regain its health.

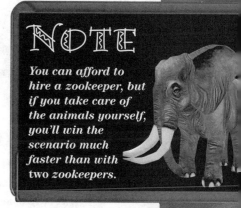

NOTE

You can afford to hire a zookeeper, but if you take care of the animals yourself, you'll win the scenario much faster than with two zookeepers.

Very shortly, you'll receive a message that everyone's totally impressed with your tycoon abilities, and that a new animal shipment has just arrived. This time it's seven chimpanzees. Like the zebras and the lions, they're dirty, thirsty, and hungry.

You receive $8,000 to develop a suitable exhibit for the chimpanzees. It doesn't really matter where you place it, since the scenario is won the moment the chimps are healed, fed, watered, and housed in a suitable exhibit. However, if you stick to the principles of economical space use in zoo design, the best spots are on the exhibit-free side of the zoo entrance, and in the area taken up by the mountain in the center of the map. It looks big and difficult to handle, but flattening it takes only seconds! Adjust the paths in the area, then stretch fencing to the exhibits on either side of your new exhibit site (see Figure 7.10). Lay down a row of food and water dishes, and repeat the procedure you've used with the lions and the zebras. That's it! You've won.

FIGURE 7.10:
The chimp exhibit fits in neatly between two existing ones. Note the row of food and water dishes waiting for the hungry animals.

SMUGGLING RING EXPOSED

Difficulty: Hard
Map: Grassland, medium
Starting Cash: $20,000
Goals:

🐾 Make sure each new animal you receive has its basic needs met.

🐾 Make sure each animal has its advanced needs met.

🐾 Release one animal of each species into the wild.

WALKTHROUGH

This scenario tests your ability to satisfy all animal needs, and to finance a quick expansion of your zoo. You'll ultimately receive seven animals belonging to seven different species. The animals arrive one by one at preset intervals; as soon as a newly arrived animal is comfortably settled in its exhibit, another animal arrives. Once all seven animals have their basic needs satisfied, you'll receive another seven—a mate for every animal already in your zoo. At this point, you will be tasked with satisfying the animals' advanced needs. When all of an animal's needs are satisfied, you may release it into the wild (the option to do so on the animal-info panel is greyed out otherwise). To win this scenario, you must eventually release one animal of each species into the wild.

As you know from Chapter 4, satisfying an animal's advanced needs includes providing stimulation (play), as well as social interaction. Many animal enrichment objects aren't available until your zoo has grown noticeably in fame, and some animals need more than a single companion to feel socially satisfied. You cannot adopt extra animals in this scenario, and you start at half-star fame. You will have to work on zoo fame to win this scenario, even though on the surface it's all about satisfying animal needs.

The starting cash you receive can be boosted considerably with recycling money: the zoo contains plenty of trees, rocks, and plants. All in all, the starting money and the recycling money are enough to build the seven exhibits required in this scenario, and even make them extra large. Use low chain-link fencing and build sunken exhibits to save a ton! You have more than enough money for high fencing, too, if that's what you must have.

The scenario begins with a single red kangaroo being delivered to your zoo. Immediately build two spacious exhibits, utilizing the front wall of your zoo as shown in Figure 7.11. Drop the kangaroo crate into the one you've chosen, and create a good scrub habitat. You'll notice that there are no trees, rocks, or plants available; you'll have to make due with the scrub biome brushes and the Create Hill and Create Valley tools. Initially, you won't be able to get foliage or rocks for many of your newly created habitats—these items will become available only when your zoo has grown in fame.

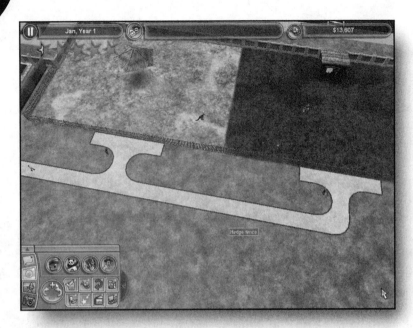

Place the first two exhibits along the zoo's front wall.

TIP

Groom every new animal right away—all of them arrive soiled from their travels, and need a good brushing.

Remember to give the kangaroo food and water. You'll also want to groom it right away. You need to wait a short while before receiving your next animal, even though all basic kangaroo needs are satisfied—be patient. You receive a Bengal tiger as your second species; put it in the exhibit next to the kangaroo, repeating the procedure. Here, too, you'll be unable to acquire any foliage for the exhibit. Remember that a tiger needs a pond in its habitat!

Making your zoo grow in fame will involve catering to zoo guests' needs, too. Fortunately, this scenario features a very nice starting layout, with a central rest and service area for the guests not far from the zoo entrance. Put down the standard starting set of guest amenities—two small restrooms, a hot dog stand, a soda stand, trash cans, etc. Place a few benches, putting a couple in front of exhibits so that guests can rest and watch animals at the same time. You'll want to research extra guest amenities later on for the boost they can give to guest happiness and thus zoo fame (see Figure 7.12).

FIGURE 7.12:

Pamper your guests; a boost in their happiness gives a boost to zoo fame.

A third animal arrives soon afterward—make sure your tiger is sated, rested, and clean as quickly as possible! This time it's a grizzly bear. Build its exhibit on the other side of the path leading to your first two exhibits. Use the zoo's side wall to save money that will let you build an extra-large exhibit. Repeat the standard procedure for new arrivals—grooming, feeding, watering. You receive a mountain gorilla next. Place it adjacent to the tiger for neighboring habitat compatibility, or use it to fill out most of the space to the right of the zoo's guest service area.

You'll receive a black rhino after the gorilla. It's one of two savannah species you'll get, so make the rhino's savannah exhibit extra large. Place it on the other side of the guest service area, to the right of the central pathway. You should have enough funds to stretch it all the way to the zoo's side wall on the right—it makes little difference in terms of money because using the zoo wall always saves a lot. Making the savannah exhibit extra big will let you put in a small lake, as well as many objects to keep the animals happy.

Place the rhino in the savannah exhibit, then groom, feed, and water it. Do not pause the game any more to build something—let the rhino run, because you need guests coming in. Since you've got several species to show right from the start, you can charge Low or Moderate admission without taking too hard a hit to your zoo fame. You should also hire a zookeeper at this time, and assign him to your first four exhibits (kangaroo, tiger, bear, gorilla). Handle the rhino

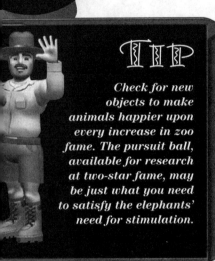

TIP

Check for new objects to make animals happier upon every increase in zoo fame. The pursuit ball, available for research at two-star fame, may be just what you need to satisfy the elephants' need for stimulation.

yourself—note that it needs to be washed pretty often. You won't have to wait long before the sixth animal arrives, hoping for a nice home in your zoo. It is an elephant, and you do not need to build anything if you've made the savannah exhibit extra large as recommended. Put the elephant together with the rhino, and boom—you've got a multispecies savannah exhibit!

The last animal is a snow leopard. Recycle the walls that form the enclosure in which the animal crates show up—this will give you enough money to build a snow leopard alpine exhibit just to the left of the zoo entrance. Groom, feed, and water the leopard; then turn your attention to tweaking your zoo to boost fame. If you haven't done it yet, research the inevitable kangaroo bouncy ride and follow up with a couple of other guest-amusement structures; don't forget about gift carts and a cotton candy cart. Get a second zookeeper to take care of the mixed savannah exhibit and the snow leopard as soon as you can afford it; i.e., when you have a steady flow of money coming in. This should happen by February at the latest; that's also when your zoo should hit two-star fame. Don't forget about family restrooms, and acquire the ice cream cart as well as a couple of guest-amusement objects.

In the meantime, all of your animals should be comfortable enough for you to receive a mass delivery: seven crates containing mates for the animals already in your zoo. Distribute the new arrivals between the exhibits as appropriate. From now on, you'll be working single-mindedly on animal need satisfaction. You must touch up the exhibits with new foliage and rock types as they become available, and make sure to get several enrichment objects for the more demanding species (gorilla, elephant). You need to have at least one animal of each species with all needs satisfied; this will let you win the scenario by releasing the happy animals into the wild. However, you shouldn't release them one by one; if you do, the single animal left behind will have its social needs unsatisfied.

There are two courses of action available to complete the final goal of this scenario. One is to monitor animal need-satisfaction levels constantly, pausing the game and releasing seven animals into the wild when it's possible to do simultaneously. The other, more elegant solution is to make the animals content enough to breed (see Figure 7.13). Once that happens, check the newborn's sex and release the older animal of the same sex after a while.

Depending on your chosen course of action, you may win this scenario as early as March, two months and a bit after scenario start. If you take the more difficult route and wait for babies to show up everywhere, you should win by June at the latest.

THE GLOBE

This campaign is the hardest in the *ZT2* Campaign game. You'll have to put to good use all the tycoon skills at your disposal to complete The Globe; the last scenario, Scarce Asian Animals, is probably the toughest one in the entire game because of the strict time limit. Completing it will unlock the globe statue.

THE WORLD'S BIOMES

Difficulty: Normal
Map: Grassland, medium
Starting Cash: $15,000
Goal:

🐾 Build a total of nine different biomes complete with animals.

WALKTHROUGH

This scenario requires you to build a total of nine exhibits, each featuring a different biome. A biome is a type of habitat plus its fauna, so each exhibit has to contain at least one animal of an appropriate species. The difficulty you'll be facing is that animals of the tropical rainforest become available only when your zoo reaches two-star fame. Note that you do not have to build a Grassland biome—the game doesn't feature grassland animals.

Winning this scenario involves building and expanding your zoo in a Challenge-game manner—except there are no challenges, and thus no extra income to be made this way. The starting cash plus the recycling money yields a grand total of around $22,000. This is enough to get your zoo off to a fast start, even when building large exhibits and adopting animals in pairs. Since you'll continue building large exhibits and generally pampering both your animals and your guests, you'll need to spend quite a lot of cash.

Begin by laying out four exhibits on both sides of the zoo entrance—the standard opening for layouts in all zoo sizes. Since money is short, consider constructing sunken exhibits, which will let you use ultracheap low chain-link

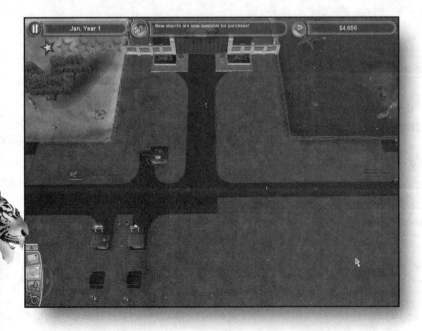

FIGURE 7.14:

New objects available for purchase!

fencing. Once the exhibits are ready, adopt the animals initially available—camel, moose, peafowl, Thomson's gazelle—extend paths and lay out viewing areas, and place the standard starting set of guest amenities. You should hit one-star fame before the month is over (see Figure 7.14).

Exceptionally sharp tycoons will be able to begin work on a new exhibit before the month is over. Sharp or not, you'll be kept busy caring for your animals—it's wise to postpone hiring a zookeeper as long as you can. Dealing with poop and emptying trash cans can make the time fly by, and one way or another you'll be adding a new exhibit in February. That's also when you can expect a wave of pregnancies, provided you did a good job on the animal habitats.

February is also when your zoo reaches two-star fame—the level necessary for winning this scenario. Improve guest amenities slightly without going overboard—remember, your goal here is to create nine different biomes. Add dessert carts and place family restrooms; research a couple of guest-amusement structures, starting with the immortal kangaroo bouncy ride. Add a hamburger stand and a water drink stand, plus a few extra benches, picnic tables, and trash cans. From now on, you'll be focusing exclusively on your animals and ignoring further guest demands. Keep an eye on trash, though; litter on the pathways of your zoo hits fame hard. You can also introduce admission fees at this time, but don't go over Moderate—you want to keep zoo fame at two-star level or better.

You should adopt gemsboks next, since they are relatively easy to care for. However, with your sixth exhibit (either ibex or emperor penguin), you'll definitely have to hire a zookeeper, even if you're Superman. You'll also need a maintenance worker. You'll be compensated by the rising zoo income; the presence of six species means six very good reasons for guests to deposit money into your donation boxes. You should complete your sixth exhibit in May at the latest. When it's done, it's time for a little coup.

As money comes in, build three small exhibits, and outfit them with the habitats that are still required by the scenario. You don't need to lay paths to these new exhibits, and you don't need donation boxes. They can actually be built anywhere you like within the zoo—you can squeeze a couple into the far corners to save money on fencing. Once the three exhibits are ready, wait until you've got enough money to adopt all the three needed species at one stroke. This time, you just need a single specimen of each species, and you don't even need to supply it with food, water, or shelter.

> **TIP**
>
> Keep switching the animals in the adoption panel to get the rather elusive ibex. You'll need the ibex for the alpine exhibit.

You'll be told you've won the scenario within seconds of placing the newly adopted species in their exhibits. Note that this cheapskate approach to winning the scenario quickly won't work well if you intend to continue playing the scenario after it's won. In that case, you should build proper, spacious exhibits for all animals, and place them according to zoo-layout rules. You should also adopt animals in pairs, and put more stress on developing guest amenities earlier in the game.

African Animal Empire

Difficulty: Normal
Map: Temperate Forest, medium
Starting Cash: $15,000
Goal:

🖐 Build a zoo containing only 12 African animal species.

WALKTHROUGH

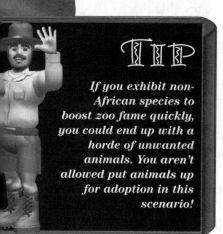

TIP

If you exhibit non-African species to boost zoo fame quickly, you could end up with a horde of unwanted animals. You aren't allowed put animals up for adoption in this scenario!

This is yet another Challenge-style scenario, but it has a wicked twist. You are to build a zoo from scratch until it contains nothing but 12 African species. To acquire adoption rights to that number of African species, your zoo must reach two-and-a-half-star fame. The catch is that there must be no other species present in your zoo.

You cannot put up any animals for adoption; you may only release them into the wild, when *all* of their needs are satisfied. So, if you aren't careful, you might end up stuck with a single unhappy peacock. You might actually have to adopt new peafowl to satisfy the single peacock's social needs so that it can be released into the wild. And if that peacock manages to fertilize a female while he's busy socializing... Remember you can't release baby animals into the wild. If you aren't careful, you could end up waiting for a long, long time to get rid of a non-African species (see Figure 7.15).

Grow up so I can kick you out!

Now that you've been warned, proceed with confidence. Begin by recycling all the trees, plants, and rocks within the zoo walls. There isn't a single tile of pathway present—you have to build everything yourself, and the extra $7,000 you get from recycling right at the start makes a big difference. You'll also receive $1,500 for every new African species in your zoo.

Your initial half-star fame entitles you to choose from four species. Two—the camel and the Thomson's gazelle—are African (remember to decline unwanted species). Build two exhibits on both sides of the entrance, and place pairs of camels and gazelles inside. Create nice habitats so that your animals are motivated to procreate. Lay down the initial path network, including a guest service area opposite the zoo entrance.

Do not attempt to build the big savannah exhibit right away. It's tempting because that's where the Thomson's gazelles rightfully belong, along with other African herbivores. But at this early point in the game, building a big exhibit is an unnecessary financial drain; the relatively small savannah exhibit required by your initial pair of gazelles can later be quickly and cheaply remodeled into a tropical rainforest exhibit for an okapi.

> **TIP**
>
> *Acquire only African species for your zoo to eliminate any problems with the release of unwanted animals into the wild. Adopt pairs initially, even though the scenario requires just single specimens. The baby animals will boost zoo fame, making up for the low diversity of species in the early days of your zoo.*

TIP

Plan to put the savannah exhibit just behind the guest service area, in the center of the zoo. Don't shed any tears if you have to erase the nice waterfall. The scenario goal is to acquire 12 African species, not to run a white-water-rafting cooperative.

Having built the two starting exhibits, set up the standard starting guest amenities in the central guest service area. You can build them relatively close to the zoo entrance, as this scenario doesn't require you to build far into the zoo. You will have plenty of money left from your initial $22,000; spend some researching the infamous kangaroo bouncy ride, and make both starting exhibits as perfect as possible. Set admission to Free before opening the zoo. You should see your fame increase to a full star by February. This lets you adopt two more African species: a gemsbok and a greater flamingo. Get a pair of both species, and make the wetlands exhibit for the flamingoes extra large—you want to fit in a crocodile and a hippo later on.

Place gift carts in strategic spots, and research the cotton candy cart. The early stages of this scenario put special stress on boosting fame through higher guest happiness, so don't be shy about spending money on barely profitable dessert carts. Add the elephant fountain to your research list, too; although its research and subsequent construction cost $800, the elephant fountain has a noticeable effect on guest happiness. Any decorative objects unlocked by completing a campaign will come in very handy! These guest-oriented moves, combined with the presence of four happy species, will quickly boost your zoo fame to one and a half stars. This, in turn, gives you adoption rights to the common zebra and the Nile crocodile; two more African species. What's more, you don't need to build new exhibits: put a single male crocodile with the flamingoes, and a single female zebra with the gazelles. You now have two multispecies exhibits, which greatly increases donation flow. Also, the presence of two new species will boost your zoo fame, letting you hit the all-important two-star threshold by the end of March. That's the right moment to start work on the big savannah exhibit in the center of the zoo (see Figure 7.16).

FIGURE 7.16:

Guest donations will skyrocket once your big savannah exhibit is complete.

You should have enough money to complete the savannah exhibit—you'll be receiving $1,500 with each new African species introduced into your zoo. Also, remember you can build a sunken exhibit and use low fencing to save money! Once the exhibit is ready, move the gazelles and the zebra inside. Add a male ostrich when you can afford it. Remodel the abandoned small savannah exhibit into a home for an okapi, and adopt a single okapi male. You now have eight African species in your zoo, and probably some baby gazelles, camels, gemsbok, and flamingoes. This alone should pump your donation boxes full of money, and push your zoo up to two-and-a-half-star fame. At this point, you can easily afford to hire a zookeeper and a maintenance worker.

If two-and-a-half-star fame is elusive, research a couple of the more expensive guest amusements (gorilla bars, hippo bouncy ride), and swap the small restrooms for the family models. Research and build a hamburger stand and a water drink stand, complete with picnic tables and trash cans. But from that point onward, resist any further entreaties to invest directly in guest happiness. Instead, focus solely on acquiring new African species. Your zoo should reach two-and-a-half-star fame by the end of May at the latest; this gives you adoption rights to no less than four African species: giraffe, lion, cheetah, and hippo. You can acquire just a single representative of each species, but it will still be very expensive.

TIP

If you have fame problems, release an older animal or two into the wild once babies are around. It gives your zoo an instant fame boost.

If you've done your job well, you should be able to charge Moderate admission prices without any danger of your fame slipping below two and a half stars. However, admission income will pale in comparison to the amounts stuffed into the donation boxes outside your big savannah exhibit (make sure you place two or even three boxes there). Begin the last series of adoptions by acquiring a giraffe and a hippo; this will further increase income from donations. You should be able to acquire a lion and a cheetah simultaneously by the end of September. Place them in the savannah exhibit with the herbivores— this wins you the scenario instantly.

North American Foreign Content

Difficulty: Hard
Map: Tropical Rainforest, medium
Starting Cash: $20,000
Goal:

> Build a zoo containing 11 animal species: three from North America, eight from other regions.

Walkthrough

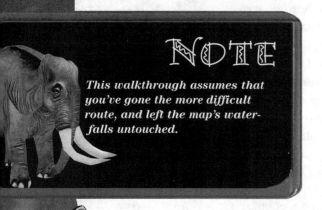

NOTE

This walkthrough assumes that you've gone the more difficult route, and left the map's waterfalls untouched.

This scenario requires you to build a zoo containing three North American species. However, your zoo must hit three-and-half-star fame before you can gain adoption rights to the three North American species in the game. To reach the required fame, you must exhibit many different species, so collecting eight non–North American ones isn't a big deal. The big deal is getting the grizzly to show up in one of the adoption slots once you fulfill the other requirements. Getting to four-star fame might be helpful simply because it opens up two more adoption slots.

The scenario features one of the most difficult maps in the Campaign game, and you should examine it carefully before proceeding with any construction. You have two choices: flatten everything, erasing the pretty waterfalls near the zoo entrance, or leave the waterfalls in place and proceed to build your zoo at the far end of the existing pathway. The scenario goals can be met while utilizing roughly half of the available zoo area; space is not a concern.

Leaving the waterfalls means leaving the existing pathway as is—you have more than enough money to get your zoo going quickly, anyway. Recycling trees, plants, and rocks adds nearly $3,700 to your starting money. You can quickly build exhibits for all of the four species available initially at half-star fame. Note that these include one North American species: the moose.

Start by flattening all the terrain beyond the waterfalls. If you do it before you begin to recycle, you won't have to rotate the map repeatedly to get at hidden objects. Extend the existing central pathway and lay out the four initial exhibits on both sides. Build sunken exhibits with low fencing to save money. Consider making the savannah exhibit for Thomson's gazelles extra large so that you can add other savannah species later without any trouble. It's simplest to stretch it all the way from the center pathway to the zoo's side wall. Leave adequate space between exhibit fences and the pathway—you'll use it for guest amenities (see Figure 7.17). Things will be a little tight, but workable. You'll be adding other guest structures later along the main zoo paths, too.

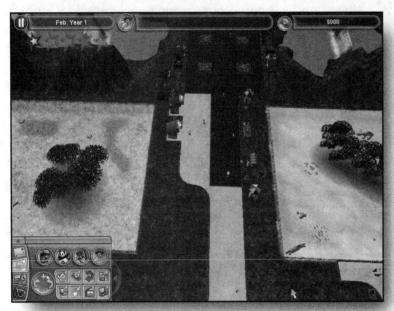

FIGURE 7.17:

Retaining the starting zoo layout makes your guest service center resemble the village High Street.

Put in the standard starting set of guest amenities to begin with, set admission to Free, and get rolling. While guests arrive, touch up the animals' exhibits without spending a fortune; remember that meticulously executed habitats reward you with more money in the donation boxes. As usual, adopt animals in pairs. Baby animals are probably the single most powerful booster of zoo fame in the game. You'll also find that releasing a few animals into the wild will help raise your fame level quickly.

Your zoo will hit one-star fame before January is over. Make sure you get only the gemsbok from the three new adoption choices, and build a spacious scrub exhibit. Placing it along the side wall next to your big savannah exhibit is a good solution. Remember that you'll be adding kangaroos later, so give the gemsboks plenty of space! Low chain-link fencing for a large sunken exhibit will cost you as little as $2,000 if you use the zoo's side wall. Add another $500 for new pathway and a donation box, and that's it! Gemsbok cost $2,000 a pop, but get a pair anyway. Babies rule!

At this point, you should use your remaining starting money to research and/or acquire a series of guest service structures. Place gift carts, research the cotton candy cart and the notorious kangaroo bouncy ride, and put benches in strategic spots. Don't go overboard; you need to start saving money for the zebras. Zebras become available at one-and-a-half-star fame, cost $3,000 apiece, and will turn your savannah exhibit into a multi-species exhibit.

> ## NOTE
>
> *As you should know by now, multi-species exhibits are cash machines for your zoo. Guests go nuts with their money upon seeing nature mix together in various attractive shapes and forms. Placing an ATM next to a large multispecies exhibit is a wise move in big zoos.*

Placing the first zebra into the savannah exhibit will push your fame to the all-important two-star level by the end of March. Turn your attention to the zoo guests; as usual, begin by exchanging small restrooms for the family model. Splurge on an insect house, and the exciting hippo bouncy ride; don't forget about the ice cream cart, and get the hamburger/water drink stand combo if you haven't done so yet. Keep checking the adoption choices while you improve guest amenities. You're hunting for ostriches (to add to the big savannah exhibit) and kangaroos (to add to the gemsbok exhibit).

March is also when the first babies will appear in your zoo, and the resulting improvement in cash flow will let you save up for the new animals quickly. You'll be pretty busy with zookeeper and maintenance worker duties by now; once you get the first kangaroo and the first ostrich, hire zoo staff. You won't even feel the bump in expenses, thanks to the extra donation money that'll come from improving one multispecies exhibit and adding another by putting a kangaroo with the gemsbok. Get the mates for the ostrich and the kangaroo next, while tweaking zoo layout to optimize the growing traffic flow.

You need to acquire only one more species at this point to display the eight non-American species specified in the scenario goal. Your next exhibit could be a Tropical Rainforest biome with a jaguar or an okapi—these are the most economical choices at this point. You may make this a single-animal exhibit to save money—jaguars and okapis aren't very social animals. But the stylish move at this point is to get a pair of giraffes for your savannah exhibit. Your fame will have reached the necessary two-and-a-half-star level by this time. Giraffes are expensive, but they are great crowd-pleasers, which directly increases donations. A pair may cost $15,000, but you'll be saving some money putting them into an existing exhibit. There is no time limit to complete this scenario, and it's a great opportunity to observe the effect giraffes have on zoo guests, even when performing such mundane activities as eating or drinking.

You now have the eight non-American species that constitute the mandatory foreign zoo content. This should bring you the three-star fame you need to acquire adoption rights for the American beaver. However, the beaver may prove elusive. Making it show up as a choice on the adoption panel may involve repeatedly declining the entire adoption lineup. You'll need $10,000 for a solitary beaver; once you've got 10 grand saved, don't be afraid to invest in guest service infrastructure. If you've got the money, go ahead and build a couple of extra exhibits for new non-American species. Remember, you need three-and-a-half-star fame before you have a shot at acquiring the grizzly bear, which is the last of the three North American species required by the scenario goal. *Four*-star fame will open up two extra adoption slots on the adoption panel. This will greatly improve your chances of actually scoring a bear or a beaver on the adoption panel (see Figure 7.18).

> ## TIP
>
> *Don't forget to check on the status of all your animals via the Quick Stats display! Help out your zookeeper(s) as appropriate, and identify animals that can be released into the wild.*

FIGURE 7.18:
Gotcha! Now all I need is four grand, and you're mine.

Your zoo should be holding steady at three-and-a-half-star fame by the end of September at the latest. If you're diligent about checking the adoption choices, you should bag a beaver and a bear by the end of the year even if you're spectacularly unlucky.

Remember, the beaver always comes first, and it requires a new wetlands exhibit. However, the bear can be placed in the existing moose exhibit. You win the scenario the moment the bear is placed in the exhibit.

Scarce Asian Animals

Difficulty: Hard
Map: Boreal Forest, medium
Starting Cash: $25,000
Goal:

   Obtain four Asian animal species within one year.

Walkthrough

This is probably the toughest scenario in the game, as it has a very strict time limit. You have to reach four-star fame well in advance of the end of the year to get the four rare Asian animals. As usual, you'll have to decline species up for adoption many times before the species you want appears. Also, the Asian species you have to acquire are very, very expensive: $15,000 for the Bengal

tiger, and $20,000 apiece for the snow leopard and the red panda. Needless to say, to reach four-star fame, you'll have to spend much, much more on other species and guest amenities.

You begin this scenario with a nice-looking little zoo that contains three exhibits. However, this is a zoo made for strolling around in guest view, and little else. The existing layout effectively cuts off one whole wing of the zoo; the camel exhibit is very poor; and the unleveled terrain makes zoo expansion a nightmare.

Your best bet is to pause the game and recycle everything, firing all the zoo staff while you're at it. This will instantly boost your starting funds to well over $40,000, which will make a very big difference to your chances of winning this scenario. Forty grand is enough to kick off the game with four exhibits and guest amenities right away, and with plenty of money left over (see Figure 7.19). Flatten the terrain before building, as recommended in Chapter 2. If you want rises and dips and winding paths, play a different scenario. Scarce Asian Animals is the supreme test of your moneymaking skills: any money you spend that doesn't meaningfully boost either your income or your fame is money wasted. If you start flinging dollars around, you may run out of cash to win this scenario (at least, without using the cheat that's revealed at the end of this walkthrough).

FIGURE 7.19:
Starting afresh with the zoo layout yields many rewards.

TIP

Make the savannah exhibit very large from the start so that you can add extra species later without any trouble.

You should have retained your starting animals when rebuilding the zoo, and added a peafowl exhibit, which will give you the first of the four Asian species. Now that they're in their new, low-budget exhibits (sunken exhibits with low chain-link fence), release one of the three female Thomson's gazelles into the wild for a little initial boost in zoo fame, then acquire mates for all the animals (all three species need mates). As usual, you want many babies in your zoo, and you need to release many animals into the wild for the fame boost.

Remember that multispecies exhibits are winners all around: guests love them and give you more donations, and they cost less per species exhibited. Plan to build three multispecies exhibits from the very start: the savannah, a wetlands exhibit combining flamingoes and crocodiles (hippos might prove too expensive), and a scrub exhibit combining gemsbok and kangaroos. Unfortunately, a big tropical rain-forest exhibit with okapis and lemurs will probably be out of reach financially (chimpanzees and gorillas definitely will be too expensive). Note that regardless of what exhibits you end up with, you'll want to acquire pairs belonging to at least 10 different species for breeding purposes so that you can easily meet animal-population requirements for four-star fame while releasing many animals into the wild.

Further zoo expansion follows the standard strategy for a Challenge game—except that there is a very tight time limit, and no extra income from winning challenges. You won't be getting any money from putting up animals for adoption, either! The right way to set about maximizing your income is to invest everything you have at the start quickly and wisely; don't hoard money at the start! Research all the new options that become available at one-star fame, and build everything that can make you any money. Add basic guest amusements and decor, then halt all expenditures until you've got $6,000 stashed away to acquire a pair of zebras the moment they become an option at one-and-a-half-star fame. You could also consider adding a penguin exhibit. Penguins cost little, but cannot use a man-made shelter—you'll have to use solid fencing or habitat features such as deep water to provide them with privacy.

You should hit two-star fame in February. Proceed to make the usual rest-room improvements, and get a compost building right away—but proceed slowly with other investments, making sure your stash keeps increasing enough for you to build a scrub or wetlands exhibit in March. You also want to acquire a pair of ostriches for the savannah exhibit. At this point, you really cannot put off hiring a zookeeper any longer. You might as well splurge the extra $200 on a maintenance worker and stop worrying about overflowing trash cans. You'll have enough on your mind already.

Babies could start appearing on the scene as early as late February; keep careful track of animal sex and age as recommended in Chapter 4 so that you release the oldest animals, and don't keep adult males you don't need for breeding purposes. You should research and acquire animal enrichment objects or toys at this time; that will most likely provide the boost you need to hit three-star fame in April or May. Get a restaurant for the guests, and touch up the animal habitats with newly available foliage and rocks. Then focus on acquiring extra species. Get a pair of gemsbok, flamingoes, kangaroos, and ibex—these are the last animal pairs you need to acquire for breeding purposes. Follow up with the jaguar and the okapi—they represent two good budget choices, and are happy enough alone, meaning you can get single specimens. Add a crocodile to the wetlands exhibit, and you should hit four-star fame.

What follows now is the Great Adoption Lottery. You will, no doubt, have declined the adoption choices many times already, but now the process will acquire a feverish intensity. You need three animals in addition to the common peafowl you acquired earlier: the Bengal tiger, the snow leopard, and the red panda. They require a total of $55,000. Fortunately, you do not absolutely need to build exhibits. If worst comes to worst, you can drop them into the appropriate existing exhibits at the last moment. The Bengal tiger can go with the jaguar in the tropical rainforest exhibit; the snow leopard with the ibex in the alpine exhibit; and the red panda with the common peafowl in the temperate forest exhibit. You may want to legitimize this move by actually releasing the existing inhabitants of the exhibits into the wild. Beware! A sudden drop in fame could lose you the red panda when the number of available adoption slots drops together with fame.

Very good players will manage to build new exhibits for the rare Asian animals. Good players will most likely win by putting the panda with the peafowl in the scenario's last month, December (see Figure 7.20).

There is also a blatant cheat that should enable almost everyone to win this scenario fairly quickly: After acquiring the Bengal tiger, play the adoption lottery until you've got both the snow leopard and

> # TIP
>
> *Reaching four-star zoo fame by the end of September is key to winning this scenario without cheating. If you can't, a delicate cheat is to save the game before each new draw in the adoption lottery, and reload the save if the species you draw aren't satisfactory.*

*Winning this
scenario involves
nail-biting
suspense as you
watch the money
counter.*

the red panda lined up. Don't despair if you see you'll be short of money. As the
zoo starts to darken and December draws to a close, pause the game and
recycle your own zoo. There's a small fortune sunk into the zoo structures, and
you should be able to raise the money you need. Acquire the snow leopard and
the panda, drop them into existing exhibits, and unpause the game to win this
scenario instantly.

CONSERVATION PROGRAMS

This campaign all about caring for animals. Playing it immediately after the
Zookeeper in Training campaign is a very wise move. The three scenarios in
Conservation Programs are all relatively easy to complete, and they play at a
relaxed pace that lets you calmly absorb many of the finer aspects of the game.
Completing this campaign unlocks the The Mysterious Panda campaign.

ANIMAL ADOPTION PROGRAMS

Difficulty: Normal
Map: Wetlands, small
Starting Cash: $20,000
Goal:

✋ Make all the animals you receive feel good enough to breed, and put
one of each species up for adoption while maintaining a thriving animal
community.

WALKTHROUGH

You begin this scenario with four pairs of animals: your starting species are ibex, beaver, cheetah, and hippopotamus. You have more than enough money to build four spacious exhibits; plan for accommodating up to six animals in each. You'll have plenty of cash left over to set up the standard starting set of guest facilities, lay out new paths and viewing areas, and immediately research the infamous kangaroo bouncy ride.

It goes without saying you must re-create your animals' natural habitats to the very best of your ability. Unfortunately, at your starting half-star fame level, you won't have access to vegetation and trees for most exhibits. Fortunately, the zoo's wetlands terrain suits two of your starting species—the hippo and the beaver. Transfer appropriate foliage and wetlands objects such as logs into your new exhibits; double-click on objects to pick them up quickly. Since you have plenty of cash, provide each species with the full range of food available, and immediately begin research of animal enrichment objects. Don't forget to build shelters!

FIGURE 7.21:
A free gemsbok! You'll have plenty of money to set up bonus animals in comfortable habitats, even though their welfare isn't relevant to winning the scenario.

Given a proper effort on your part, you should begin getting news about animal pregnancies within a month. Here's the deal: you must put up for adoption one animal of each species. Its sex isn't important. Each new species you put up for adoption nets you a cash grant of $2,000 (not that you need it). What's more, you'll receive one animal of a new species for the first three species you put up for adoption (see Figure 7.21). For example, putting up two cheetahs and one ibex for adoption will give you two new animals: one for the cheetah, one for the ibex. The fourth new species put up for adoption isn't rewarded by a new animal—it wins you the scenario instead.

Since you must maintain a thriving community for each species, there's a wait involved—especially because of the hippos, whose gestation periods and childhoods are much longer than those of the other three involved species. You'll most likely offer several beavers and cheetahs for adoption before you can offer a single hippo! Expect to win this scenario somewhere around the half-year mark.

Animal Conservation

Difficulty: Normal
Map: Tropical Rainforest, small
Starting Cash: $20,000
Goals:

- Meet all needs of the mountain gorillas, red pandas, and snow leopards that are donated to your zoo, and ensure that they breed.

- Collect $7,500 in guest donations for each of the three donated species.

Walkthrough

This fairly easy scenario has a nice starting setup; the existing pathways are helpful in developing your zoo quickly. You're not pressed for space or time, even though it's a small map. Your zoo will contain a maximum of five exhibits, and you shouldn't have a problem fitting them in.

Begin by quickly constructing three exhibits for the crated animals, making sure there's plenty of space for future offspring. Use the roundabout around the pond in the center of the zoo as the hub for your path network (see Figure 7.22). This scenario emphasizes balancing traffic flow between your exhibits. You want the $7,500 in donations to accumulate reasonably in step for all three species. Start by putting two adjacent exhibits left of the center path, and your guest service area and the third exhibit to the right. Of course, you'll be using zoo walls as usual to save a lot of money on fencing.

FIGURE 7.22:

Plan your zoo around the existing round-about.

Use the existing tropical rainforest foliage and rocks to trick out the gorilla exhibit. Unfortunately, your low fame won't allow you to finish off the red panda and snow leopard habitats with rocks and vegetation. Provide plenty of space, and a balanced mix of biome brushes for each exhibit (don't forget about shallow water!). Equip each exhibit as well as you can, and immediately begin researching enrichment objects. The small ball and scratching post both work well at keeping your animals reasonably happy. If you've done the job well, everyone and their aunt will be getting pregnant in February. Expect the babies to arrive a month later (see Figure 7.23). The arrival of the first baby panda, leopard, or gorilla usually coincides with the donation of a new animal to your zoo in March. Use the new species to balance traffic flow— it will probably make sense to put it next to your existing solitary exhibit and guest service area.

FIGURE 7.23:
It's a boy! The presence of baby animals will, as always, have a considerable impact on guest donations.

From March onward, you'll be focusing on collecting money in donation boxes. If necessary, boost the fortunes of the less popular exhibits by hiring educators dedicated to these exhibits. An educator instantly boosts the flow of donation money! Also, research popular guest attractions such as the insect house, and place them by the exhibit that could use extra guest traffic. Remember to monitor the donation flow by selecting the Donations by Species tab on the donation-box panel.

After that, it's a matter of sitting back and watching the money come in. Expect to win this scenario around the middle of the year.

NOTE

Your zoo receives three new animal donations in this scenario. The animals arrive at preset intervals of around two months. Think twice before building exhibits for the new animals: you do not want to interrupt the flow of donations for the animals that matter in this scenario.

SECOND GENERATION ANIMALS

Difficulty: Normal
Map: Grassland, medium
Starting Cash: $20,000
Goal:

☞ Breed at least one grandchild from the animals you receive at the start.

WALKTHROUGH

This pleasant and easy scenario completes the Conservation Programs campaign. Playing it should finely hone your skill at caring for animals. The most important lesson you'll learn is this: always build bigger exhibits than you think you'll need.

You're given more than enough money to build three very large exhibits without having to recycle anything. However, you only need two: a savannah exhibit for the zebra, and a tropical rainforest exhibit for the chimpanzees and the lemurs. As usual, it's simplest to put them to both sides of the zoo entrance, extending the fence all the way to the zoo's side walls. Put the crossroads right under the diamond-shaped guest service area that comes with the zoo. Finish off the two exhibits as well as you can (you won't have access to any foliage or rocks for the tropical rainforest habitat), set up the standard starting guest amenities, and set the admission to Free before unpausing the game and opening the zoo! Free admission and low food and drink prices boost guest happiness, and guest happiness has a meaningful impact on zoo fame.

> ## TIP
>
> *Work on zoo fame in this scenario, because higher fame will eventually unlock the exotic vegetation and rocks you need for your exhibits, along with better animal toys. Increasing fame is difficult because of the low number of species in your zoo (although you'll get some miraculous assistance there).*

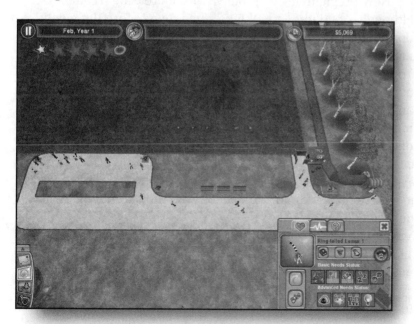

FIGURE 7.24:

Now look at all those nice menu choices I have—who cares if there are no trees in the restaurant?

Giving your animals the best care possible is priority number one. To this end, you should hire a zookeeper right away—you can afford one as well as a maintenance worker from the very start. If you've built nice, big exhibits and modeled them well, your animals will soon be in top form in spite of the lack of foliage and rocks (see Figure 7.24). And happy animals always mean a constant flow of money into the donation boxes—this is the mainspring of financial success in the game! Never forget that.

You'll get news of animal pregnancies by the end of February. The first babies should follow in March; a month later, you will receive the first of several animal donations to your zoo. Note that the animals given to you may be of the same species as the ones you have; if so, put them in the relevant exhibits, where they'll increase the frequency of pregnancies. However, in the beginning, a different species is more helpful since it will boost zoo fame far more strongly. Don't delay in setting up an exhibit! Recycle some of the starting zoo objects if you've spent a lot of cash on zoo decor and research in your efforts to increase guest happiness. One way or another, you should be able to afford an exhibit right away. Place it across the path from the zebra exhibit. The mixed chimp/lemur exhibit tends to draw most of the zoo's guests right away, and placing an exhibit in the other wing of your zoo will balance traffic.

TIP

Keep upgrading the Savannah and Tropical Rainforest biomes with new foliage and rocks when they become available. Research and add all-new enrichment objects, too—you want your animals as happy as possible.

New pregnancies will follow with increasing frequency, although, of course, it will take some time before the newly born animals grow old enough to have kids. If you haven't made your exhibits extra big, you'll be forced to do so now! You can expect several pregnancies and births a month on the average, and you'll also be getting increasingly frequent free animals for your zoo—the more pregnancies and births, the more new arrivals. Build additional exhibits around the diamond-shaped guest service area (you may have to trim it a little); such exhibit placement will pull traffic in a third, new direction. This is also the time to expand guest amenities. You'll reach two-star fame by April, and two-star fame always means rapid zoo expansion thanks to the many new choices that become available.

All these activities will keep you fairly busy, but don't become too busy to check on your animals. Chimps, particularly, need plenty of attention; you'll be grooming one or another almost constantly—they get dirty quickly, and when they get dirty, they fall ill. The last thing you want is sickness and death of one of the potential grandparents!

If you stay on top of things, you can expect an animal born in your zoo to become pregnant by the end of July. Now all you need to do is run things efficiently for another month and a bit, and you've won this scenario. You may still get one or two free animals at that time; don't bother building exhibits for them unless you intend to play the scenario even after you've won it. It's not the best choice for extended play, though.

THE MYSTERIOUS PANDA

This stand-alone scenario is one of the two ultimate tests of your tycoon abilities (the Scarce Asian Animals scenario is the other). You're given a very generous budget to work with, and there's no time limit. The scenario goal means you'll have to build a zoo of five-star fame—that's the requirement for getting adoption rights for giant pandas. You'll also have to upgrade the habitats continuously as new objects become available. The educational qualities of your habitats have a significant impact on your zoo's fame, and you'll need to get the giant panda's habitat exactly right to motivate it to reproduce.

Completing this scenario unlocks the gilded panda statue.

Difficulty: Hard
Map: Grassland, medium
Starting Cash: $100,000
Goal:

🐾 Breed giant pandas in your zoo.

WALKTHROUGH

You'll be spending the first few minutes of this scenario on pause; you'll want to expend part of the $100,000 in starting money on immediately setting up four exhibits for all the animals available at half-star fame. Dedicate one wing of your zoo right away to the mammoth savannah exhibit—it has to be big enough to contain half a dozen species, including rhinos and elephants! It's a good idea to make it L-shaped (see Figure 7.25). Put the desert habitat for the camel next to the savannah to capitalize on terrain compatibility. As you know from Chapter 4, animals do take note of the neighborhood, and placing compatible habitats next to each other is beneficial. You need to take advantage of every little nuance to reach five-star fame!

FIGURE 7.25:
This is the easy way to lay out the extra-big savannah exhibit required in this scenario.

TIP

Acquire animals in pairs (at least the first 10 species) for breeding purposes. You'll need to release many animals into the wild to reach five-star fame!

When you've finished the first three exhibits, laid down the paths, and set up basic guest amenities, unpause the game and acquire the fourth species for your fourth exhibit. Thereafter, proceed to develop your zoo as you would in a Challenge game, but with one difference—hire a zookeeper and a maintenance worker right away. You have plenty of starting money, and if you use low fencing and sunken exhibits, you can continue building new exhibits and adding guest amenities without pause for the next few months. This will keep you too busy to worry about animal poop. Focus single-mindedly on quickly bringing your zoo up to three-star fame (don't forget to add zebras, giraffes, and ostriches to the savannah exhibit!). That's approximately when the initial zoo cash will start running low. However, by the time you've fine-tuned work assignments among zookeepers and touched up the habitats with newly available items, you'll find you've got enough cash to continue expansion.

Keep adding new species until you max out the contribution this can make to zoo fame, monitoring your progress on the Zoo Fame panel. Remember that the more species you have, the easier it is to max out the "diversity of species" component of zoo fame. Once you've reached that point, finalize your zoo layout by building new guest service areas in the rear half of your zoo. Place exotic species in the far reaches of the zoo to draw guests; given that your savannah exhibit is near the entrance, it's a good idea to put the big multispecies tropical rainforest and wetlands exhibits at the other end. That's also the zoo area where you should place rare and endangered species such as the snow leopard and the red panda. You might have to acquire some very expensive and exotic species in your bid for five-star fame, regardless of how many species you already have in your zoo.

TIP

Red and giant pandas are happy to share the same exhibit if it's big enough. You might want to build a really big exhibit for red pandas, and just add the giant panda later.

You should check the Zoo Fame panel frequently to monitor your progress. If you acquired animals in pairs, as recommended throughout this guide, you won't have a problem exceeding the needed number of animals in your zoo, and subsequently releasing enough animals into the wild to max out zoo fame in that area. Guest happiness reaches maximum shortly after you reach two-star fame and acquire the guest-related zoo objects made available at that fame level. And after you reach three-star fame and have access to its wide array of new habitat items—trees, plants, rocks, animal toys—you'll quickly meet the needed animal happiness level. The two areas of concern that will remain are the contribution to zoo fame made by educational habitats and entertaining animals, respectively. You won't have to hit 100% with either, but expect to put in a lot of work adjusting the habitats—refer to Chapters 4 and 5 and Appendix A for advice on how to cater to the terrain preferences of the game's animal species.

TIP

Research and build a compost building as soon as it becomes an option at two-star fame. It's going to make you a lot of money in this scenario!

You'll also find that a zoo of this size requires plenty of zookeepers. Don't even try to manage things yourself—as mentioned, get a zookeeper and a maintenance worker right from the start. You'll be raking poop anyway—a savannah exhibit containing half a dozen species including rhinos and elephants manufactures enough to keep several zookeepers constantly busy.

If you don't manage to get the exhibits exactly right, reaching five-star fame may involve exhibiting all the 29 species available before the giant panda. Fortunately, you have all the time in the world to tweak your zoo to perfection. You can expect a minimum of around $20,000 a month in net profit from a zoo that exhibits 25 species or more, and sharp tycoons who have read the preceding chapters will find ways of increasing this to around $30,000. A few reminders: a good mix of guest amenities, including benches and a restroom in all strategic spots, will boost your income. Add educators in front of the multispecies exhibits, and don't forget to use them as guest magnets to draw visitors into the less frequented corners of your zoo. Remember, you can relocate an educator's podium anywhere!

You should finally reach five-star fame around March of the second year. However, your zoo will show an annoying tendency to slip back to four and a half stars—all it takes is a couple of really dirty exhibits. Add new zoo staff and tweak your zoo still closer to perfection to keep fame even at five stars. You'll probably have to wait another month or so before you have the funds to adopt a male panda—it will set you back $50,000. Of course, you should have an extra-large, luxury exhibit ready first, complete with a dedicated zookeeper. Remember that giant pandas need both a lot of care and a lot of privacy, but are happy to share an exhibit with red pandas.

If you focus on satisfying your giant panda's needs, they should all be met within a short period of time. The moment they are, you'll receive a message: thanks to your newly proven skill in meeting giant panda needs, another zoo is donating a *female* panda named Li Ming. You now have a pair of giant pandas! Make sure you groom the newly arrived female, and remember to build another hollow-tree-stump shelter. Then just focus on keeping both pandas' needs satisfied.

After all the pandas' needs have been met, a pregnancy is just a question of time (see Figure 7.26). You will have so much money coming in at this point that you'll be able to afford a small army of extra zookeepers so that you can focus almost exclusively on the giant pandas' well-being.

FIGURE 7.26:
A baby panda! Being witness to this event means you've become a true tycoon.

If you do well, you can expect the newborn panda to arrive around the middle of the second year of this scenario. Most likely, this will mean you've completed the *Zoo Tycoon 2* Campaign game. Congratulations!

APPENDICES

THIS SECTION CONTAINS FOUR APPENDICES THAT WILL HELP YOU IN YOUR QUEST TO BE THE WORLD'S BEST TYCOON. THE INFORMATION THEY CONTAIN RANGES FROM GAME STATS TO INSIDER TIPS FROM BLUE FANG, THE GAME'S DEVELOPERS. HERE'S WHAT YOU'LL FIND IN EACH APPENDIX:

APPENDIX A CONTAINS ANIMAL, BIOME OBJECT, AND BIOME COMPATIBILITY DATA IN TABLE FORM. IT'S VERY HELPFUL IN DECIDING WHICH ANIMAL TO ADOPT, AND WHEN.

APPENDIX B LISTS THE GAME'S GUEST-ORIENTED STRUCTURES AND OBJECTS, THE ZOO FAME LEVELS AT WHICH THEY BECOME AVAILABLE, AND RELATED DATA SUCH AS RESEARCH, PURCHASE, AND UPKEEP COSTS FOR EACH STRUCTURE AND OBJECT.

APPENDIX C LISTS THE CHALLENGES YOU MAY ENCOUNTER WHEN PLAYING ZOO TYCOON 2 IN CHALLENGE MODE. IT INCLUDES COMMENTS ON CHALLENGE DIFFICULTY AND THE REWARD YOU RECEIVE WHEN YOU WIN A CHALLENGE.

APPENDIX D CONSISTS OF TIPS FROM GAME INSIDERS AT BLUE FANG AND MICROSOFT GAME STUDIOS. MAKE SURE YOU CHECK THEM OUT! THEY AREN'T REPEATED ELSEWHERE IN THE GUIDE.

VISIT THE SYBEX WEB SITE AT WWW.SYBEX.COM FOR MORE ON ZOO TYCOON 2!

APPENDIX A: ANIMAL, BIOME OBJECT, AND BIOME COMPATIBILITY DATA

ANIMAL DATA

The first table contains useful animal data:

Space per animal (first/subsequent animals): the first animal in an exhibit always needs much more space than the subsequent ones.

Guest attraction (adult/baby animals): this value indicates how many tiles a guest is prepared to walk to see an animal when deciding which exhibit to visit next. Note that a guest may notice an animal from a pathway, but will move to a viewing area if it offers a better view (is closer to the exhibit).

Maximum donation: this indicates the maximum amount that a guest can donate after being impressed by an animal. Note that if a guest is standing near the donation box, he may donate money even though you don't see the donation animation taking place onscreen.

Adoption chance: this is the chance that a given species will appear in a vacated adoption slot. The higher the number, the *lower* the chance this will happen.

Life Span: this is the animal's life span in game months. Reaching this value does not mean automatic demise for an animal. Instead, every so often there is a chance the animal will die of old age. Lucky animals may live longer than their life span value.

Reproduction chance; size of litter: reproduction chance is the chance that mating will result in a pregnancy; in *ZT2*, all pregnancies are successful. Size of litter shows the number of possible offspring.

Can swim: this indicates whether the animal can swim. Swimming helps satisfy an animal's need for exercise, and some species need deep water in their habitat (see Chapters 4 and 5). Don't include deep water in exhibits containing animals that can' swim!

SPECIES	SPACE PER ANIMAL (FIRST/ SUBSEQUENT ANIMALS)	GUEST ATTRACTION (ADULT/ BABY ANIMALS)	MAXIMUM DONATION	ADOPTION CHANCE	LIFE SPAN	REPRODUCTION CHANCE; SIZE OF LITTER	CAN SWIM
Bear, Grizzly	80/20	50/55	$100	70	43	75%; 1–3	Yes
Bear, Polar	80/20	50/55	$100	70	31	75%; 1–3	Yes
Beaver, American	70/10	50/55	$100	60	13	75%; 1–3	Yes
Camel, Dromedary	70/10	0/5	$60	1	43	75%; 1	No
Cheetah	90/30	20/25	$80	50	16	75%; 2 or 3	Yes
Chimpanzee	50/3	60/65	$100	70	51	55%; 1 or 2	No
Crocodile, Nile	70/10	0/5	$60	30	60	75%; 1 or 2 (eggs)	Yes
Elephant, African	80/20	60/65	$100	80	69	55%; 1	Yes
Flamingo, Greater	50/3	0/5	$60	20	8	75%; 1 (egg)	Yes
Gazelle, Thomson's	50/3	0/5	$60	1	13	75%; 1	No
Gemsbok	70/10	0/5	$60	20	17	75%; 1	No
Giraffe, Reticulated	50/10	15/20	$80	50	24	75%; 1 or 2	No
Gorilla, Mountain	70/10	60/65	$100	80	39	45%; 1 or 2	No
Hippopotamus	70/10	20/25	$80	50	39	75%; 1	Yes
Ibex	70/10	20/25	$80	30	19	75%; 1 or 2	No
Jaguar	70/20	15/20	$80	40	19	75%; 2 or 3	Yes
Kangaroo	70/3	5/8	$60	40	17	75%; 1	No
Lemur, Ringtailed	50/3	20/25	$80	60	21	75%; 1 or 2	No
Leopard, Snow	80/25	80/85	$120	80	16	45%; 2 or 3	Yes
Lion	50/12	20/25	$80	50	21	75%; 2 or 3	Yes
Moose	70/10	0/5	$60	1	23	55%; 1–3	Yes

SPECIES	SPACE PER ANIMAL (FIRST/ SUBSEQUENT ANIMALS)	GUEST ATTRACTION (ADULT/ BABY ANIMALS)	MAXIMUM DONATION	ADOPTION CHANCE	LIFE SPAN	REPRODUCTION CHANCE; SIZE OF LITTER	CAN SWIM
Okapi	70/15	50/55	$100	40	21	55%; 1	No
Ostrich	50/5	0/5	$60	40	34	75%; 1 (egg)	No
Panda, Giant	80/20	100/150	$120	100	26	25%; 1	Yes
Panda, Red	50/5	80/85	$120	80	12	55%; 1 or 2	No
Peafowl, Common	50/3	0/5	$60	1	17	75%; 1 or 2 (eggs)	No
Penguin, Emperor	50/3	15/20	$80	20	34	75%; 1 (egg)	Yes
Rhinoceros, Black	80/20	30/35	$80	60	39	45%; 1	No
Tiger, Bengal	70/20	30/35	$80	70	15	75%; 2 or 3	Yes
Zebra, Common	50/3	0/5	$60	30	24	75%; 1	No

TREES, PLANTS, AND ROCKS: AVAILABILITY BY FAME

This table shows the fame levels required to unlock specific trees, plants, and rocks (in that order). It is helpful when deciding whether to adopt a certain species, and lets you plan future adoption choices. Note that this table does not enumerate various kinds of decorative plants (medium purple flowers, bed of tulips, etc.).

BIOME TYPE	HALF STAR	ONE STAR	TWO STARS	THREE STARS	FOUR STARS
Alpine	none; none; none	Himalayan pine tree; larkspur; none	none; none; small rock	yellow cedar tree; none; medium rock	Himalayan birch tree; none; large rock
Boreal Forest	balsam fir tree; reindeer lichen; small rock	none; fringed polygala flower; medium rock	tamarack tree, red cedar tree; none; none	black spruce tree; none; large rock	none; none; none
Desert	camel thorn acacia tree; desert grass; small rock	date palm tree; protea wildflowers; medium rock	none; none; large rock	none; none; none	none; none; none
Grassland	none; dandelions; small rock	trembling aspen tree; june grass, sedge grass, decorative flowers; large rock, medium rock, small rock	none; new decorative flowers only; none	none; new decorative flowers only; none	none; new decorative flowers only; none
Temperate Forest	maple tree; none; none	none; lily of the valley; small rock	none; none; none	birch tree; white lilies; medium rock	none; fountain bamboo, water bamboo; large rock
Tropical Forest	none; none; none	none; none; none	kapok tree, tree fern; none; small rock	foxtail palm tree, kily tree; toadstools, African violets, banana leaf plant; medium rock	banana tree, elephant ear tree, orchid tree; jungle lilies; large rock

BIOME TYPE	HALF STAR	ONE STAR	TWO STARS	THREE STARS	FOUR STARS
Tundra	none; none; none	none; arctic moss; small rock	none; none; none	none; none; medium rock	none; none; large rock
Savannah	umbrella acacia tree; African daisies; small rock	none; none; medium rock	baobab tree; blackthorn bush; none	acacia caffra tree; elephant grass; large rock	none; none; none
Scrub	none; none; none	weeping myall tree; spinosa bush; small rock	none; bluebush; medium rock	yellow fever acacia tree; none; large rock	none; none; none
Wetlands	none; none; none	mangrove tree; cattails, small wetland log; small rock	cypress tree; water lilies, gamba grass; medium rock	none; wetland log, papyrus; large rock	none; none; none

ANIMAL/BIOME COMPATIBILITY

This table shows the compatibility between animals and the different biome types. Use it when choosing a location for a new exhibit to minimize potential conflict between biomes that are greatly different. For instance, you would not want to place a grizzly in a boreal forest exhibit adjacent to a desert exhibit. Ten is the perfect value for a species' native biome; the smaller a value, the bigger the conflict between the species and the type of biome.

SPECIES	BIOME TYPE									
	ALPINE	BOREAL FOREST	DESERT	GRASSLAND	TEMPERATE FOREST	TROPICAL RAINFOREST	TUNDRA	SAVANNAH	SCRUB	WETLANDS
Bear, Grizzly	2	10	-10	0	0	-5	0	0	-5	-5
Bear, Polar	2	0	-10	0	0	-10	10	-5	-5	-5
Beaver, American	-5	0	0	0	2	-5	-10	2	2	10
Camel, Dromedary	-5	0	10	2	0	-5	-10	2	2	-5
Cheetah	-5	0	0	0	2	0	-10	10	2	-5
Chimp-anzee	-5	0	-5	0	2	10	-10	0	0	0
Crocodile, Nile	-5	0	0	0	2	-5	-10	2	2	10
Elephant, African	-5	0	0	0	2	0	-10	10	2	0
Flamingo, Greater	-5	0	-10	2	0	0	-10	2	0	10
Gazelle, Thomson's	-5	0	0	2	0	-5	-10	10	2	-5
Gemsbok	-5	0	2	0	0	-5	-10	2	10	-5
Giraffe, Reticulated	-5	-5	0	0	2	-5	-10	10	2	-5
Gorilla, Mountain	-5	-5	-5	0	0	10	-10	0	-5	0
Hippo-potamus	-5	0	0	0	2	-5	-10	2	2	10
Ibex	10	2	-10	0	0	-5	2	-5	-5	0
Jaguar	-5	0	-5	0	0	10	-10	0	-5	0
Kangaroo	-5	0	2	0	0	-5	-10	2	10	-5
Lemur, Ringtailed	-10	-5	-10	2	2	10	-5	0	-5	0

SPECIES	BIOME TYPE									
	ALPINE	BOREAL FOREST	DESERT	GRASSLAND	TEMPERATE FOREST	TROPICAL RAINFOREST	TUNDRA	SAVANNAH	SCRUB	WETLANDS
Leopard, Snow	10	2	-10	0	0	-5	2	-5	-5	0
Lion	-5	0	0	0	2	0	-10	10	2	-5
Moose	5	10	-5	3	6	-5	2	-5	-5	5
Okapi	-5	-5	-5	0	0	10	-10	0	-5	0
Ostrich	-5	0	0	2	0	0	-10	10	2	-5
Panda, Giant	0	2	-5	0	10	0	-10	-5	-5	-5
Panda, Red	0	2	-5	0	10	0	-10	-5	-5	-5
Peafowl, Common	2	-5	-10	-5	-5	-5	10	-5	-5	-5
Penguin, Emperor	2	-5	-10	-5	-5	-5	10	-5	-5	
Rhinoceros, Black	-5	-5	0	2	2	-5	-10	10	0	0
Tiger, Bengal	-5	2	-5	0	0	10	-10	-5	-5	2
Zebra, Common	-5	0	0	2	0	0	-10	10	2	-5

Appendix B: Buildings, Structures, and Objects by Fame

Fame: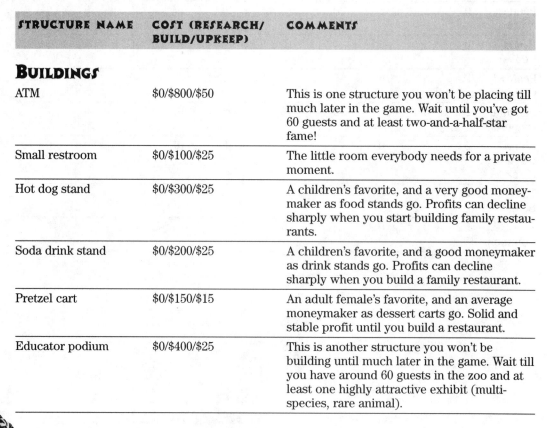

STRUCTURE NAME	COST (RESEARCH/ BUILD/UPKEEP)	COMMENTS
BUILDINGS		
ATM	$0/$800/$50	This is one structure you won't be placing till much later in the game. Wait until you've got 60 guests and at least two-and-a-half-star fame!
Small restroom	$0/$100/$25	The little room everybody needs for a private moment.
Hot dog stand	$0/$300/$25	A children's favorite, and a very good money-maker as food stands go. Profits can decline sharply when you start building family restaurants.
Soda drink stand	$0/$200/$25	A children's favorite, and a good moneymaker as drink stands go. Profits can decline sharply when you build a family restaurant.
Pretzel cart	$0/$150/$15	An adult female's favorite, and an average moneymaker as dessert carts go. Solid and stable profit until you build a restaurant.
Educator podium	$0/$400/$25	This is another structure you won't be building until much later in the game. Wait till you have around 60 guests in the zoo and at least one highly attractive exhibit (multi-species, rare animal).
STRUCTURES AND OBJECTS		
Donation box	$0/$200/$0	Place one per standard viewing area, two per large viewing area, and one at each busy crossroads.
Trash can	$0/$100/$0	On average, you need two per food/drink stand. Place some by the stands, some in or near eating areas, plus extra ones as necessary.

Bench	$0/$125/$0	This is one of the most important items in your zoo. Place them everywhere, choosing strategic spots such as near food stands, at the rear of viewing areas, or next to restrooms.
Picnic table	$0/$150/$0	The standard seating for guests consuming food and drink in your zoo.
Kangaroo bouncy ride	$200/$300/$0	The first in a long line of bouncy rides that keep children amused.

FAME:

STRUCTURE NAME	COST (RESEARCH/ BUILD/UPKEEP)	COMMENTS

BUILDINGS

Gift cart	$0/$350/$15	The greatest little moneymaker in the game. Place one by each exhibit so that guests exiting the viewing area pass by.
Hamburger stand	$200/$300/$25	A favorite with children, and the best of the food-stand moneymakers. Profits can decline very sharply after you build a family restaurant.
Water drink stand	$200/$200/$25	A favorite with adult guests, male and female. It's a solid and stable moneymaker, though profits decline somewhat after you build a restaurant.
Cotton candy cart	$200/$100/$10	A favorite with children, and a very good little moneymaker in the early game. Profits can decline sharply after you place ice cream carts and/or build a family restaurant.
Popcorn cart	$200/$100/$10	A favorite with adult males. Profits are poor, and become dismal when you build a fancy restaurant.

STRUCTURES AND OBJECTS

Recycling bin	$0/$150/$0	This handsome green bin actually brings in a tiny profit from recycled containers. Place one after building a water drink stand.
Binocular stand	$400/$300/$0	Research the binocular stand instantly and outfit every viewing area in the zoo with at least one, preferably two. Binocular stands greatly increase guest satisfaction and stimulate donations to your zoo.
Viewing canopy	$400/$200/$0	Guests prefer to view animals from under a viewing canopy.
Marble arch	$200/$300/$0	This decorative object provides amusement for adult guests.
Elephant fountain	$400/$400/$0	This decorative object provides amusement for adult guests.

FAME:

STRUCTURE NAME	COST (RESEARCH/ BUILD/UPKEEP)	COMMENTS

BUILDINGS

Family restroom	$0/$300/$25	This building revolutionizes guest service in your zoo. It basically makes progress possible. Build in guest service areas and near very busy crossroads.
Compost building	$400/$1,000/$50	This is a surefire investment that should be made every time you play a longer game.
Insect house	$800/$1,200/$100	Expensive but necessary! The insect house is very helpful in satisfying the amusement needs of all zoo guests. Don't be afraid to build more than one.
Animal photo booth	$400/$500/$50	Expensive and unnecessary. This amusement is aimed at adult guests, who rarely feel the need to visit it when strolling through an aesthetically pleasing zoo.
Sub stand	$400/$300/$25	This is a favorite with adult males, and a respectable moneymaker until you build a restaurant.
Coffee stand	$400/$600/$25	This is a favorite with adult guests, male and female. It's a really good moneymaker until you build a fancy restaurant.

Salad stand	$400/$300/$25	This is a favorite with adult females, and an average to good moneymaker throughout the game.
Ice cream cart	$400/$200/$15	This is a favorite with children. Very good initial profits can decline when you place an ice cream cart, and can drop further when you build a family restaurant.

STRUCTURES AND OBJECTS

Umbrella table	$600/$150/$0	The preferred outdoor seating for your zoo guests. Use umbrella tables to replace picnic tables.
Lamp post	$0/$125/$0	A decorative object pleasing to adult guests.
Wooden viewing canopy	$600/$200/$0	Guests prefer to view animals from under a viewing canopy.
Polar bear statue	$600/$300/$0	A decorative item appreciated by adult guests.
Wooden arch	$600/$300/$0	A decorative object appreciated by adult guests.
Music rock	$600/$100/$0	A decorative item liked by all your zoo guests. Walk nearby to hear the theme tune!
Hippo bouncy ride	$600/$300/$0	A new-generation bouncy ride for your child guests.
Gorilla climbing bars	$600/$300/$0	A playground that satisfies the amusement needs of your child guests.

FAME:

STRUCTURE NAME	COST (RESEARCH/ BUILD/UPKEEP)	COMMENTS

BUILDINGS

Staff center	$0/$500/$50	A place for zoo staff to gather when there is no work to be done. It's unnecessary unless your ambition is to run a social club for zoo staff.
Gift shop	$800/$800/$50	An excellent moneymaker that should be placed in guest service areas only.
Shetland pony ride	$800/$1,400/$100	A very good moneymaker if placed in a high-traffic area. Recommended location: the guest service area in the front half of your zoo.

Shishkebab stand	$800/$800/$25	A favorite with adult males, and an average to poor moneymaker that starts to lose money after you build a fancy restaurant.
Sushi stand	$800/$800/$25	A favorite with adult females, and an average moneymaker throughout the game.
Cheesecake cart	$800/$400/$20	A favorite with adult males, and an average to good moneymaker until you build a fancy restaurant.
Fruit cup cart	$800/$400/$20	A favorite with adult females, and an average to good moneymaker until you build a restaurant.
Family restaurant	$800/$500/$100	A favorite with children, and an excellent moneymaker, but it kills food-stand profits nearby. You never need more than two, and most often just one.

STRUCTURES AND OBJECTS

Zoo map	$0/$250/$0	A decorative object appreciated by adult guests.
Steel viewing canopy	$800/$200/$0	Guests prefer to view animals from under a viewing canopy.
Rhino statue	$800/$300/$0	A zoo-decor item pleasing to adult guests.
Lion fountain	$800/$400/$0	A zoo-decor item pleasing to adult guests.
Lion bouncy ride	$800/$300/$0	A new-generation bouncy ride to amuse your child guests.
Rhino bouncy ride	$800/$300/$0	Yet another super-duper bouncy ride that pleases child guests.
Gazebo	$800/$150/$0	A decorative zoo structure appreciated by adult guests.

FAME:

STRUCTURE NAME	COST (RESEARCH/ BUILD/UPKEEP)	COMMENTS

BUILDINGS

Reptile house	$1,000/$1,200/$100	A favorite with all zoo guests. Research and build it as soon as possible; don't be afraid to build more than one (depends on the number of insect houses, too).
Restaurant	$1,000/$500/$100	A favorite with adult guests, and a very good moneymaker, but it sharply cuts the profits of all adult-focused food stands.
Fancy restaurant	$1,000/$1,200/$100	A favorite with adult guests, especially males, and an average to very good moneymaker, depending on other food establishments in your zoo.

STRUCTURES AND OBJECTS

Stone viewing canopy	$1,000/$200/$0	Guests prefer to view animals from under a viewing canopy.
Stone arch	$1,000/$300/$0	A decorative structure appreciated by adult guests.
Tiger fountain	$1,000/$400/$0	A decorative structure appreciated by adult guests.

APPENDIX C: CHALLENGES

PHOTO-SAFARI CHALLENGES

All of these involve fun with the camera, but the later challenges can be very hard to complete.

EASY PHOTO-SAFARI CHALLENGES

Gardening Society challenge excepted, all easy photo-safari challenges are good opportunities to get your zoo going quickly in the early game.

BUILDING DESIGN

Zoo Design, Inc. is running a trade piece on maximizing guest amenities and is particularly interested in your zoo's offerings. They will mention your zoo in their article, boosting your zoo fame, if you provide them with pictures of some of your amenities. You will need to photograph the following amenities:

- Gift cart
- Kangaroo bouncy ride
- Small restroom
- Any food stand

Reward: Small boost to zoo fame.

Comments: This is a very nice challenge because you're sure to have all three required structures in your zoo (and if you don't, you should get them right away). Naturally, your zoo has to have one-star fame so that the gift cart is available. Remember that even a small fame boost is immensely helpful in the early game!

GARDENING SOCIETY

The Gardening Society is interested in your display of plant life and has asked you to make a presentation about the foliage in your park. They will pay you $2,000 for your appearance. To support your presentation, you will need four photographs of plant life from four different regions of the world, where each picture shows the foliage displayed in its appropriate biome. The presentation will increase public awareness by appealing to an audience that may not be aware that your zoo offers more than just animals.

You'll need foliage from the Savannah, Tropical Rainforest, Boreal Forest and Alpine biomes.

You need to provide photos of the following trees:

- Baobab: Savannah, Africa

- Kapok: Tropical Rainforest, South America

- Tamarack: Boreal Forest, North America

- Himalayan Pine: Alpine, China

Reward: $4,000. You'll hear your presentation was such a success that it was repeated, and as a result you get double the promised money.

Comments: This is a very nice and easy challenge *if* your zoo has reached the two-star fame needed for all of the trees to become available.

PROMOTIONAL PHOTOS

The marketing department is preparing a new zoo brochure and has requested pictures of the following:

- A guest holding an ice-cold soda

- A guest sitting on a bench

Providing these pictures will help improve your zoo fame as flyers promoting your zoo begin to circulate around your community.

Reward: A small zoo-fame boost (less than half a star).

Comments: This is a very easy challenge; you might be able to win by taking a single photo if you don't have picnic tables and guests are forced to sit down on benches in order to consume what they bought.

SCIENTIFIC JOURNAL

You have been approached by a scientific journal writing an educational piece about even-toed ungulates (Artiodactyls). They have requested 3 specific pictures for their article and have offered you $750 per picture. If you can provide a picture of a dromedary camel, a gemsbok and a Thomson's gazelle, you will be paid $2,250. The publicity will also provide a bonus to your zoo fame.

Reward: $2,250 and a small fame boost

Comments: If you have all the three species required in your zoo, go for it! If not, pass—unless you're missing just one species that you've been planning to add anyway.

WILDLIFE PHOTOGRAPHY LESSON

The Alfred Windsor School of Photography would like you to provide a photo for it to use as a sample in the wildlife-photography segment of its curriculum. The school needs only one photograph, but to make it more interesting for the students, it should be a snapshot that contains at least two animals. In return for this photograph, the school will present you with the Alfred Windsor Photography Award of Merit, which you can display as an example of your efforts to help the community. You will also receive a $2,000 licensing fee.

Reward: $2,000 and a nice award

Comments: This one's a walkover. If you've been adopting animals in pairs as recommended throughout the guide, cashing in on this challenge will take 30 seconds. If not, it will take 60 seconds; you have to pick up an animal from any exhibit and place it next to another animal in another exhibit. Snap—and it's done.

MODERATE PHOTO-SAFARI CHALLENGES

These challenges are more difficult, but still reasonably easy to complete provided your zoo features the required animals.

CENTER FOR ANIMAL CONSERVATION CONTEST

The Center for Animal Conservation has issued an open contest to obtain pictures of endangered animals. Winners will receive the Animal Conservation Image Award and a cash bonus of $15,000. The required animals are Bengal tiger, snow leopard, mountain gorilla, and grizzly bear.

Capture one picture of each of the following animals to qualify for the award.

- Bengal tiger
- Snow leopard
- Mountain gorilla
- Grizzly bear

Reward: $15,000 and a nice award

Comments: You need four-star fame to complete this challenge. Naturally, it helps if you already have all four of the required animals in your zoo. If you're missing just one, think hard about acquiring it and taking on the challenge. All four of the species highlighted by this challenge are very attractive to zoo guests.

EL BISTRO MAGAZINE

El Bistro Magazine wants a unique angle for an upcoming issue and would like to feature photographs of animals eating from interesting containers. They have requested photographs of a cheetah, a reticulated giraffe, and a ring-tailed lemur eating from specific food containers and will pay you $2,000 per photo.

Provide the following photographs:

🐾 A cheetah eating meat from an artificial carcass

🐾 A reticulated giraffe eating branches from a browse holder

🐾 A ring-tailed lemur eating from an elevated food dish

Reward: Total of $6,000

Comments: This challenge requires three-star zoo fame. If you've got the animals in question, go for it, buying the fancy tableware if necessary. Many zoos built on medium and small maps won't have the cheetah because of its extravagant space requirements. If that's your situation, pass on this challenge.

NATIONAL ZOO ASSOCIATION

The National Zoo Association is running a contest among all member zoos and will award all participants with a $5,000 grant. They have requested 2 pictures of rare zoo events. Specifically they are looking for a photo of any animal baby with its mother and any animal making use of an enrichment object.

You need photographs of:

🐾 Any animal baby with its mother

🐾 Any animal using an enrichment object

Reward: $5,000. This is quite a lot of money in the early-to-middle game, and usually enables you to adopt a new species plus build a new exhibit.

Comments: If you've followed the advice in this guide, you won't have a problem taking a photo of a baby animal with or without its mother. Obtaining the second photo is a little more difficult: you have to let the animals get somewhat dirty before they'll use the scratching post (the most common enrichment object in the early stages of the game).

SCIENTIFIC JOURNAL FOLLOW-UP ARTICLE

You have been approached by the scientific journal for a second series of pictures on the dromedary camel, gemsbok, and the Thomson's gazelle. They will pay you $1,500 per picture for photographs that capture these animals performing specific activities.

Capture these animals performing the following activities:

🐾 A dromedary camel grooming another camel

🐾 A gemsbok sleeping in the shade

🐾 A Thomson's gazelle greeting another gazelle

Reward: A total of $4,500

Comments: It's money for nothing! Let the camels get a little dirty, and you'll have no trouble getting the first snap. You might have to remove the gemsbok's shelter to get the second picture reasonably fast. The third snap is also easy to get: Thomson's gazelles are very social animals. Remember to watch animal status (the middle tab on the animal-info panel) to see what an animal is up to.

ZOO NEWS MONTHLY

Zoo News Monthly wants to run an article on your zoo but needs pictures to back up their story. Once you provide the photos, they can run the news piece, which will have a positive impact on your attendance for the next 3 months that the issue is displayed on the news stands. They are looking for photos of:

🐾 A jaguar swimming in the water

🐾 An ibex resting in a stable

🐾 A moose rubbing its antlers on a tree

Reward: One-time boost in zoo attendance following completion of the challenge

Comments: Take on this challenge only if you have all the species required in your zoo, *and* can afford the time to stalk your moose; its picture isn't easy to get. The swimming jaguar pic is easy if you cheat a little by picking up a jaguar and dropping it into deep water.

CHALLENGING PHOTO-SAFARI CHALLENGES

These challenges are truly tough, and completing them all takes a lot of patience.

ANIMAL ENRICHMENT

A national conference has scheduled a session on the topic of psychological stimulation for animals in captivity. You have been offered a spot on the interactive panel segment and have been asked to provide photographs to support

the discussion. You will be paid $20,000 if you participate and provide photographs of the required animals interacting with specific enrichment objects.

Capture photographs of the following:

- A polar bear using a car tire

- An African elephant using the easel

- A Bengal tiger lying on a heated rock

- A black rhinoceros playing with a pursuit ball

Reward: $20,000

Comments: This four-star-fame challenge isn't easy to complete even when you've got all the required animals and enrichment objects. The exhibits concerned are likely to be far apart (even if your elephants and rhinos live together). A four-star zoo is big and has plenty of events, yet you'll have to spend considerable time waiting to pounce on your animals with your camera. Naturally, it helps to remove all other enrichment objects from the animals' exhibits, but even then, things may take a while. However, the extra $20,000 is nice (it roughly equals a four-star zoo's monthly net income).

ANIMAL INSTINCTS

A group of ethologists will be visiting your zoo to further their studies of animal instinctual behaviors. To help make their visit more time-efficient, they have asked you to capture images of certain behaviors. If you can accommodate their request, they'll share their knowledge of animal behaviors with your guests and boost your zoo fame. You will need to capture photographs of ring-tailed lemurs, a pride of lions, ostriches and reticulated giraffes.

Capture photographs of the following animal behaviors:

- A ring-tailed lemur grooming another lemur, satisfying social and hygienic instincts

- A pride of lions consisting of one adult male, three females and one young lion

- An ostrich doing a mating dance

- A young giraffe calling to its mother

Reward: A boost in zoo fame

Comments: This challenge is hard to complete. You need to have quite a few lions in your zoo, plus a baby giraffe and a pair of ostriches; and catching a male ostrich performing its mating dance can prove difficult. Naturally, it's best to give it a pass if you haven't got all the necessary animals in your zoo.

BECKENSPOT PRIMATE

A school group will be taking a field trip sponsored by the Beckenspot Charitable Foundation to visit the primates in your zoo. The Foundation would like souvenir photos to give to each of the students as a reminder of their visit. They have asked you to provide specific photos of mountain gorillas and chimpanzees. In return for your efforts, they will present you with the Beckenspot Charitable Foundation Photographic Portfolio Award at a black-tie awards ceremony recognizing benefactors of the Foundation. The publicity you will receive at this well-heeled event will provide a significant boost to your attendance.

Photograph the following animal behaviors:

🐾 A mountain gorilla chuckling

🐾 A male mountain gorilla calling to his troop

🐾 A chimpanzee using the monkey bars

🐾 A chimpanzee climbing a tree

Reward: A boost in zoo attendance

Comments: This is a difficult challenge, even when you've already got both gorillas and chimps in a multispecies tropical rainforest exhibit. You'll have to spend a while monitoring their behavior closely. Note, however, that a gorilla can "call to his troop" even when there are no other gorillas present in the exhibit.

HIGH CLASS DEMONSTRATION

The local high school is currently studying the concept of the food chain. They would like to demonstrate this concept to the class and have asked if you can provide a sequence of pictures demonstrating how the food chain works. They will be sure to spread the word to other schools about the help you have provided and this will enhance your attendance. You will need to set up an exhibit where a carnivore can hunt its prey.

Take a two-picture series that shows a predatory animal:

🐾 Hunting its prey

🐾 Catching its prey

Reward: A one-time boost in zoo attendance upon successful completion of this challenge

Comments: Take this challenge if you aren't squeamish. The reward isn't much, and winning this challenge takes some time and effort: it requires an

exhibit with high, strong fencing such as steel bars, because your hungry predator may try to escape! You need two animals: a predator and a "prey" animal—for example, a Thomson's gazelle and a lion. Put them together in the exhibit with high fencing, and *do not* provide any food for the predator (lion). Do provide water and otherwise satisfy the two animals' needs. Keep a watchful eye on animal status in the predator's animal-info panel so that you know when it's about to stalk and attack its prey. The new exhibit can be remodeled cheaply into a new home for any species.

GAME CHALLENGES

These are challenges that do not involve taking photographs. Often, there is more to them than immediately meets the eye. As explained below, there are some tricky choices.

EASY GAME CHALLENGES

The easy game challenges aren't all easy, but they're all fun. Note that you cannot win anything at all in Garbage Strike. The Free Admission challenge is an absolute winner when trying to get your zoo off the ground on a limited budget.

ANIMAL SALE

You've been approached by another zoo that is interested in obtaining one of your animals. In exchange for your animal, they have offered to make a generous donation to your facility. Would you like to release your (random animal) to this facility in exchange for their donation of (X dollars)?

Reward: The money offered for your animal varies, depending on the species. Is it worth it? Not always.

Comments: This one is simple. Check the price, check whether you can do without the animal in question, and decide.

ANIMAL TRADE

The Zoological Cooperative Association (ZCA) is running a feasibility study to determine if member zoos can benefit from a program of trading species between zoos. As a member, you will exchange one of your species for a new species for a temporary one-month period. It is essential that you keep the new species healthy and achieve a donation income of $500 for your new species over this period. Otherwise, the venture will be financially unsuccessful. The study will determine if a regularly rotating exhibit cycle has a positive impact on zoo attendance and cash flow. If the venture proves to be a success, you will receive $2,500 for your efforts, and you will be able to keep the new animals.

Should you accept this challenge, the species on loan will be delivered crated near your front gate. At the end of this trial period, your original species will be returned to your zoo.

Reward: $2,500 and a new species for your zoo. The actual number of animals received always equals the number of animals taken from your zoo.

Comments: This is a two-tiered challenge. You may keep the animals on loan healthy but still fail to raise $500 in donations. However, you can make sure you get the necessary donations by hiring an educator and putting the educator's podium right in front of the exhibit with the new animals. If you want to make *absolutely* sure you win this challenge, temporarily get rid of the viewing areas by neighboring exhibits.

Free Admission

Your local city council and animal welfare society want to run a "Free Admission" promotion at your zoo for community residents. They hope to deliver the message that proper care and feeding is essential to all animals, and that domestic animals deserve the same attention as the exotic animals in your zoo. They have agreed to pay you an up-front fee of $2,500. This promotion will last for up to one month as long as your animals remain healthy. At the end of the promotion period, if no animals became ill, you will receive an additional $2,500 and additional compensation for your lost admissions fees. If an animal becomes ill, the promotion will end immediately. You'll receive no further compensation and the animal will be removed from your facility.

Reward: A total of $5,000 *and* reimbursement for all admission money lost during the challenge period

Comments: This is an excellent opportunity to make a lot of money quickly early in the game. It goes without saying that your animals are receiving top-notch care, so basically all you do is change the admission to Free.

Garbage Strike

The National Refuse Collectors (Union) NRCU has just voted to go out on strike! Pending the satisfactory negotiation of a new contract, your maintenance workers have walked off the job. It is expected that the strike action could last one month. You can pay a high-priced strike team $4,000 to handle trash cleanup until your maintenance workers return. Or, you can choose not

to pay their fee, and collect and clean the trash in your zoo yourself to avoid unhappy guests. Would you like to hire the strike team?

Reward: The moral satisfaction of defeating the strikers, and managing to keep the zoo operational and profitable

Comments: There's no way to avoid this challenge—a strike is a strike. You can easily handle the trash yourself, but only if you aren't also personally responsible as zookeeper for many exhibits. Even then, it's much cheaper to hire one or two extra zookeepers than to hire the strikebreakers. Try to handle the trash yourself!

RAFFLE

The Health and Husbandry Association, a non-profit organization, is holding a 50/50 raffle and has offered to sell you a block of 10 tickets for (X dollars). Their portion will be used to benefit the health of domestic farm animals nationwide. Would you like to participate in the raffle?

Reward: Depends on the ticket price, but if you win, the reward is always nice. For example, 10 tickets bought for $1,000 wins you $4,000. This challenge appears multiple times during a game; if you lose the first time, you might win the next time around.

RANDOM NEW ANIMAL

You have the opportunity to obtain an animal that has been rescued from an illegally run animal "mill." The species has not been disclosed and your cost will be ($3,800 or $16,000) dollars to ship the animal to your facility. While it is likely that the animal is in the Lower Risk category, there is also a good chance that it is vulnerable or endangered, in which case it would be a valuable acquisition. Should you accept this opportunity, your crated animal will be delivered to the area near your front gate. Provide a suitable environment for your new animal.

Reward: A random new species in your zoo

Comments: This challenge is a bit of a lottery. If the random new species can be adopted at zoo fame of two and a half stars or less, you'll be asked to pay $3,800. If adopting the new species requires higher fame than two and a half stars, you'll be asked to pay $16,000. To come out ahead, you need to get at least a two-star-fame animal for $3,800, and at least a four-star-fame animal for $16,000. If you've been expanding your zoo in an organized manner, you'll likely have all the cheaper species already, and the random animal is always a new species. If you don't have all the cheap species, you might find out you paid nearly $5,000 for a moose. Do you feel lucky?

MODERATE GAME CHALLENGES

These challenges aren't easy, and the rewards aren't as good as in the Easy set. Animal Companions is great, but Venture Capitalist is a trap that may force you to restart your game.

ANIMAL COMPANIONS

An internationally funded conservation group has offered to send you an animal to allow you to set up a breeding situation. The cost to obtain this (random species) is (X dollars). You may keep the animal for two months. If you successfully breed this animal within the time limit, the conservation group will issue a refund for your initial cost and the animal plus baby are yours to keep. Should you fail to successfully breed this animal, the loaned animal will be returned to its owner and no refund will be issued. Finally, if the animal meets with misfortune while in your care such that it cannot be returned to its owner, you will be forced to pay (X dollars) penalty.

Reward: You're set up with a breeding pair of animals.

Comments: You know how to care for animals so that they breed, don't you? Go for it! The risk is practically nonexistent. You'll pay the fine only if the animals fail to breed *and* cannot be returned to the conservation group (because you gave them up for adoption, for instance).

ENRICHING ANIMALS

The Residential Family Society has begun a campaign promoting the benefits of enrichment and stimulation for preschool children and is making the correlation that captive animals also benefit from enrichment and stimulation in their lives. They have issued a challenge to zoos nationwide to provide their animals with ample enrichment objects, and have imposed a one-month deadline.

Since your zoo is local to their headquarters, they have targeted your facility for extensive publicity. You will need to research six new enrichment objects and use them in your exhibits to demonstrate your commitment to animal enrichment.

If you succeed, you will benefit from free publicity and a boost to your attendance. Should you fail to uphold their ideal, they will be merciless in their criticism and you will likely see your attendance decrease.

Reward: Increased zoo attendance and a small boost to zoo fame. If you fail, you'll suffer decreased fame and zoo attendance!

Comments: Do you actually have six enrichment objects that you can research right away? If not, getting more means your zoo has to become more famous first. It's very difficult to guarantee that within one month, and the penalty is severe. Don't take this challenge unless it's in the bag!

BEAR CONFERENCE

Bear biologists from around the world are looking for a venue where they can hold a conference to share the latest research and management information about bears. They have agreed to hold their conference at your site and pay you a $2,000 site fee as long as you can add another species of Ursidae to your facility. According to the terms they have presented, you must have another species on-site within four months. If you fail, you will need to pay them a $3,000 cancellation fee.

Reward: $2,000

Comments: This challenge is worth it only if you've already got both the grizzly and the polar bear in your zoo, or if you have one and intend to acquire the second shortly anyway. A paltry $2,000 doesn't make much difference to a zoo that has reached three-and-a-half-star fame (required for the grizzly).

VENTURE CAPITALIST

You've been approached by a venture capitalist who is certain that there is a buck to be made in creating a top-notch zoo. He's ready to provide $10,000 in immediate funding. You will need to repay him at a rate of 40% of your donation income, up until the point where he has achieved a gain of $2,000 over and above his initial investment.

Reward: New financial wisdom

Comments: With your donation income slashed by 40%, repaying the loan is gonna take a very long time—and throughout that time, you'll be paying, paying, paying…. This isn't even loan sharking, it's extortion. Avoid this one. It can cripple zoo development.

CHALLENGING GAME CHALLENGES

There are two challenges in this group—one nice, one not so nice. You can't win with Animal Stress unless you count the loss of thousands of dollars in revenue as a victory. Animal Release, on the other hand, isn't terribly hard and carries a proper reward.

ANIMAL STRESS

A national zoo inspection agency has filed a complaint against your facility, citing that animals at your facility have been subjected to "behavioral stress and unnecessary discomfort." If you argue their claim, your zoo will be closed to the public for one month while they re-inspect the facility for ill or unhappy animals. If you do argue the claim and the animals are again found in poor condition at the end of the month, you will pay a $2,500 fine. If you do not argue the charge, your zoo will remain open to the public but you will be unable to adopt any new animals for one month. Do you wish to argue the claim?

Reward: None. Whichever way you look, you lose. You'll get $5,000 if the inspection agency investigates the claim and finds it unjustified, but that's always much less than the money you lose when your zoo is closed for a month.

Comments: It's likely you'll never see this challenge, because it occurs only if your animals are in poor shape. If it *does* occur, don't argue with those pinheads. Closing the zoo for a month may mean tens of thousands of dollars down the drain. Pass on adopting new animals for one month, and make sure you improve your animal care!

ANIMAL RELEASE

An internationally funded conservation group has offered you an incentive to release endangered animals to the wild in an effort to promote growth among old populations and make new populations of these animals self-sustaining. Their current research project involves the (random species). You have been offered (X dollars) to prepare your (random species) for release into the wild. (X dollars) will be paid up front, and the remainder will be paid when the animal has been collected for its relocation to its natural habitat.

Reward: A nice sum of money—the more exotic the species concerned, the more money you get.

Comments: Do you have the needed species in your zoo, or intend to acquire it very soon? If so, go for it. If you're following the advice in this guide, breeding animals in your zoo is easy, and you need to release just one to win this challenge.

VARIABLE GAME CHALLENGES

The two challenges in this group vary in difficulty depending on the random choices the game makes.

ANIMAL AWARENESS DAY

The board of directors of the National Animal Association has sent out a request to zoos nationwide. (Random species) Awareness Day is two months away and they would like all member zoos to have at least one animal of this species on-site within that time period. Their promotional campaign will be extensive and if you have one of these animals in your zoo within two months, you will benefit not only from increased attendance but also from the (X dollars) cash grant available to all participating members.

Reward: A grant that varies according to the species of animal chosen for Awareness Day. The increased attendance is always a great boost, though, and you might see it increase slightly even if you fail to get the new species for your zoo.

Comments: Everything depends on the species that were chosen for Awareness Day. If you don't have the new species and can afford it, go for it! The increased attendance alone will pay for it eventually.

SPECIAL GUEST

You've received a tip that the CEO of a prominent and very wealthy corporation is planning to visit your zoo in the upcoming months. You've heard that your important guest's favorite animal is the (random species), and the rumor is that if this animal is in your zoo when your VIP visits, it is likely that you will receive a generous donation.

Reward: The more exotic the species required, the bigger the donation.

Comments: Do you have that species in your zoo, or intend to acquire it anyway? If so, great. If not, pass up this challenge; you'll get another shot at it later in your game.

APPENDIX D: DEVELOPER TIPS

This appendix contains selected tips from the designers and testers at Blue Fang Games and Microsoft Game Studios. Is there anyone who knows the game better than these guys? Probably not.

Bart Q. Simon, Senior Designer, Blue Fang Games:

When you raise the admission price, guests have to be more impressed by your animals to donate a given amount of money. Lowering admission price means you can get higher donations for the same animals than you would when admission price is high.

When guests satisfy a need, they do a flat analysis that compares their needs against all potential satisfiers. Their need level, how much they "think" the satisfier will meet that need (favorite foods come into the picture here), distance to the satisfier—all these factors play a role. The guest then chooses to go to the satisfier that has the greatest post-computation value.

Carnivores will attack prey animals when they are hungry. If you keep a carnivore well-fed in an exhibit with prey animals, they will not attack the prey. Male animals of the same species will fight as their reproduction need gets higher. This is to simulate the territoriality between males in an animal population.

Guests get tired over time and will want to rest, but slopes won't tire them more than flat ground. Viewing animals makes guests tired, too.

If you see an animal that's having trouble satisfying its Privacy needs, simply pick it up and move it to a shelter, or a secluded spot.

Linda M. Currie, Senior Designer, Blue Fang Games:

Hold the Shift key down to run around when in first-person-view mode.

Place food and enrichment objects within a few tiles of your guest view areas. This will make sure animals are frequently in view of the guests as they satisfy their needs.

Place gift carts and gift shops near the animals that they sell trinkets for. Guest who have just enjoyed watching the chimps may be more inclined to purchase a chimp-related gift. And if a building isn't getting much traffic, you're better off bulldozing it and trying it somewhere else.

Animals are affected by the terrain outside their exhibit area, so don't put polar bears next to your gorillas, because their biomes clash. It's a good idea to avoid building long, thin exhibits for the same reason.

Remember that you can decline a photo challenge any time, even when you've already started taking the pictures.

Val Miller, Software Test Engineer, Microsoft Game Studios:
The sundial that you unlock by completing the Prevent Animal Abuse scenario is a very good object to get early in the game. It's compact, so it's easy to place, and gives adult guests a good boost towards satisfying their Amusement need.

Want to skip to each exhibit area easily? Just take one of your zookeepers and assign them to all the exhibits—that way, you can select that zookeeper to open their info panel, and from there, jump to each assignment flagpost quickly and effortlessly.

Staff gates are very, very handy things—when dropping down into Zoo Guest mode to take care of tasks yourself, note the areas where you'd like to pass through—and put a staff gate on that fence section to make traversing your zoo that much easier. It works especially well when there are several exhibits sharing fence lines.

Animals can drink water placed by the biome brush in a pinch, saving you a bit of cash, and it doesn't require refills—just watch out: some animals have trouble even in shallow water, so keep an eye on them when they go to take a sip.

Some animals even sample some of the plants in their exhibit when hungry—place some native foliage in animal exhibits, and it might disappear in an area full of hungry herbivores.

Don't like the animals available in the Adoption panel in Campaign or Challenge mode? Don't decline any just yet—first save the game when all the slots are full. After saving, decline all the animals you don't want; if the one you do want doesn't appear next to fill the slot, simply reload the save game to give it another whirl—this is a quick and dirty way of finding the animal you want.